# Ribbons of Highway
## A Mother-Child Journey Across America

To Carol,
Enjoy the journey —
All the best,
Lori Hein
12/12/04

Printed in the United States of America

Booklocker.com
2004

# Ribbons of Highway
## A Mother-Child Journey Across America

**Lori Hein**

*To Mike, my partner in making all life's dreams come true*

# About the Author

Lori Hein is a freelance writer whose work has appeared in local, regional and national publications. She is also a features correspondent for several Boston-area community newspapers. A marathoner, she does some of her best writing while running. This is her first book.

Before turning to writing full-time, she spent over 20 years in the corporate world in sales, marketing, training, and organizational development.

She is a world traveler who has journeyed to over 50 countries, capturing impressions of the world's places through journals and photography.

A *magna cum laude, Phi Beta Kappa* graduate of Tufts University, Lori also studied at the Sorbonne in Paris and earned an MBA from Suffolk University.

Lori lives in the Boston area with three Belangers – husband, Mike, and kids Adam and Dana.

She can be reached at LHein10257@aol.com.

# Table of Contents

# *Introduction*

Although my kids and I didn't climb into the van and drive off until nine months later, our 12,000-mile American road odyssey began on September 11, 2001.

Where I was and what I was doing when the planes ripped through New York are part of my life's fabric. I was outside painting the fence brown, telling my neighbor Donna that I'd plenty of time now to do the job my 13-year-old son was supposed to have finished because I'd just been laid off. We groused about the economy's sorry state and mused over whether things could get any worse.

In the next instant, they did. The kitchen phone rang. It was my husband calling from the car to tell me one of the twin towers had been hit. Mike was on the road, making sales calls, and hadn't seen any pictures yet. He'd only heard the radio reports.

The paintbrush hardened outside in the sun, pieces of cut grass sticking up like spikes in the brown mess.

When Adam and Dana came home from school, we gathered around the table on the deck, and began, as a family, to sort through facts and feelings and fears. The kids' teachers had done a good job dispensing comfort and assurance before sending them home. By the time they got to us, we'd decided we had three things to communicate: they were safe and loved; America was strong; the world's people were good.

To our family, this last point was as important as the others, because our kids have been traveling the world since they were babies. Respect for the world's people is part of their upbringing. This is a gift, and we'd allow no senseless act, however brutal, nor any retaliatory distrust or intolerance, to steal it.

My mind's eye called up images: two Turkish teenagers kicking a soccer ball with a 5-year-old Adam on the grounds of Topkapi Palace; Adam joining a group of Bolivian boys in tabletop foosball during recess at Copacabana's school, Lake Titicaca shining at the end of the street; the kids building sand castles with Javier and Daniel, two Belizean brothers who'd pass our hotel each day on their way to class; Dana setting off for a bird walk, in the shadow of Kilimanjaro, with Mike and Masai chief Zapati. These experiences enrich life and must continue.

As the painful, numbing slowness of the weeks immediately after September 11 yielded to something approximating normalcy, I regained enough focus to give the future some thought. That future had us traveling again, but this time, we'd get to know our America.

# 1

## *GETTING READY*

"Can I start packing?" asked Dana. Such an exuberant little ball of energy, she thought the road trip idea was colossal and couldn't wait to stuff her backpack. It was September. We were leaving in June, right after school let out. "It's a little early, Dane, but start making a list of things to bring. Or, start making a pile of things you think you want to take." She knew the pile strategy. Before every trip, a pile of definite-and-maybe gear grows on the rug in the TV room. It's my staging area. "Will we need plastic spoons?" "Maybe. Put them in the staging area." Pile up now, pare down later.

At first, Adam saw the idea of an American road trip as two months away from his friends, locked in a van with his mother and little sister. It's not that he didn't want to go .He just didn't want to be gone "so long." A reasonable reaction from a 13-year-old.

His vision of this rolling summertime hell persisted intermittently until the June afternoon when key met ignition, and we left our Boston area neighborhood behind. We'd find that, once the deed was in motion, Adam would truly enjoy most of it. And I would enjoy him enjoying it.

There was a lot to do to get ready, so I was in my element. Few things thrill me more than piecing together a trip, and this one was a biggie. I plunged into the planning like a carnivore into sirloin.

The staging area sprouted seeds in January, and, by March, grew too big for the TV room. I moved it to the basement exercise area, leaving a small path for the back and forth slices of the NordicTrak's skis. Most of the stuff in the pile came from Wal-Mart. We went at least a dozen times. The kids loved these expeditions. The first time, though, I went alone and completed a three-hour, aisle-by-aisle, item-by-item reconnaissance mission. Would we need this? Could we use that? If we didn't have one of these, would we be sorry? If we had one of those, would the trip be safer, more fun, more organized, more comfortable?

For three months, the NordicTrak sliced through the Wal-Mart mountain. We had notebooks and pens; a tent; Sterno; a windshield sunshade; pots; bungee cords; folding tables; beach chairs; sunscreen; bug juice; flashlights; batteries; film; tape of all kinds; clamps of all sizes; plastic sheeting; sleeping bags; Ziploc bags; Brillo pads; pot holders; baby wipes; utensils; safety flares; jumper cables; water jugs; wiper fluid. Hundreds of items, large and small, amassed to face the final cut to determine what went and what didn't.

I'd already pared down my original route plan, an out-by-the-south and back-by-the north string of back roads and byways I'd highlighted in yellow and pink in the Rand McNally road atlas. Some things – indeed, some whole states and regions – had to go. If I didn't, with regret, cut out the Cahokia Mounds, Galveston, White Sands and the sidewalk egg-fry in Oatman, Arizona, we'd be on the road so long I'd have to homeschool the kids in the van. Phileas Fogg circled the globe in less time than it would have taken us to get to Sioux Falls.

We zoomed in on a seven-week trip length and agreed on a collective must-see list. Dana had to have Kentucky horse country. Adam didn't really care, as long as he saw "car museums" and had plenty of snacks. I wouldn't negotiate away Appalachia, Cajun country, New Mexico's pueblos, Monument Valley, the Avenue of the Giants, Idaho, the Tetons or the Great Lakes. The reworked itinerary boiled down to 51 days. Sold.

Armed with a rough outline of our route, I went online and ordered every applicable town, city, county and state brochure and map in print. When they came, I filled out every reply card and sent away for more. My mailman, Tom, spent months bent under the weight of those deliveries. He caught me, in early June, in a van-packing practice run.

"So, you're heading out."

"Yep, in two weeks."

"Any chance you've got room for my son?"

"Maybe I could stuff him up top, in the Thule."

"That'd be good."


I'd pored over every map and brochure Tom had delivered over the months, and had strung together a route that tied scores of small ribbons of highway together into a complete odyssey. We would take interstates only when they were unavoidable or, when, in the interest of ensuring we'd be home by mid-August, we simply needed to make time.

Though I used the Rand McNally and all the state maps that Tom had delivered to plan the route, and brought them all with us on the trip, I would navigate by a document I called the Route Narrative. After my children, my journal, my Nikon and my wallet, the Route Narrative would become the next most important piece of cargo.

I took all the yellow and pink highlighted lines I'd drawn on the scores of planning maps and turned them into words. I didn't want to fool with the folding and unfolding of maps. I wanted one simple tool that would tell me where to head next and how to get there. And, I wanted something I could hold, so I could feel, at once and not in pieces, the pull and power of a whole nation. I wanted to hold the entire country in my hands, every morning before we set out and every night before we went to bed. I wanted a thrilling, perfect, complete thing.

The Route Narrative took our 12,000-mile quest and distilled it down into a three-page series of transcontinental run-on sentences written in the imperative, with verbs that got my blood up. Commands like go, take, follow, get on, pick up, cross and continue.

The five days and thousand miles between Tahoe and Crater Lakes thus became: "Take 20W at Emigrant Gap and continue through Nevada City and Grass Valley. Stay on 20W, crossing much of the state, to intersection with Route 101 (also Route 20) at Calpella. Take 101/20N to Willits, where 101 goes north and 20 goes west. Take 20W at Willits to Route 1 and head south on 1 to Mendocino. After Mendocino, take 1N along the coast to 101N at Leggett (Drive-Thru Tree Park). Stay on 101N to Phillipsville, where get on Avenue of the Giants that parallels 101 for 33 miles to Pepperwood, through Humboldt Redwoods State Park. At Pepperwood, get back on 101N and stay on through Scotia, Fortuna, Eureka, Arcata, Trinidad, Orick/Redwoods Park and Crescent City to Oregon border. Stay on 101N up the Oregon Coast to Florence. From Florence, take 126W to Eugene. From Eugene, take I-5S through Cottage Grove to Roseburg, where pick up 138E to Crater Lake."

I read and reread the finished Route Narrative. America came alive in my hands. I wanted to live these words and numbers. I wanted to leave now. I wanted to meet these ribbons of road whose beginnings and ends, curves and nuances, altitudes and intersections I had studied and traced, and whose numbers flashed in my mind as I tried to sleep - numbers like 14, 39, 53, 98, 184, 267, 666.

But there were things I needed to learn before we left. Things only a Luddite needs to learn. Things that amazed people who knew me. I'd driven the Jordanian desert alone, run a marathon, packed off to China for a week of solitary exploration, been successful in business. But I couldn't pump gas, had never used an ATM (had no PINs to my name), and didn't know how to turn on a cellphone. The things that worried me about this trip- which, because of the kids, required I be in touch and ready for anything- were not the 12,000 miles, the seven weeks, the remote roads or the blistering desert, but cellphones, ATMs and gas pumps.

I bowed to progress and learned to push the right buttons. I'd sold a six-part series about the trip, to be filed from the road, to a local newspaper, so I learned to connect my laptop to the Internet without breaking the bank. Mama was wired and getting ready to roll.

Memorial Day came and went, and we turned the calendar to June. Time to tie up all preparatory loose ends. I turned New Paint, our Nissan mini-van, over to Don Borgeson for a day. Everyone should have as honest a mechanic as Donny. He checked the van from top to bottom, as if his own wife and kids were going to cross the country's most blistering lows and vertical highs in it. For $130, he declared her ready for anything. (Like any good ship, our van is a she, and she has a name. New Paint succeeds Old Paint, who served us for a decade before her retirement.)

I'd studied New Paint's interior geometry and knew every nook, cranny, angle and orifice that could possibly accommodate stuff. I bought clear plastic boxes and labeled them: mom's clothes; kids' clothes; toiletries & first aid; cooking supplies. My goal was to run our rolling house according to the maxim, "A place for everything and everything in its place." The boxes stacked snug inside the tailgate behind the rear seat.

5

I filled two cardboard cartons with food. At home, we're an organic family. I put that on seven-week hold, knowing we'd eat what we'd eat, which would often have to be a can of something brought down from the rooftop Thule and eaten cold or heated over Sterno. I bought food my kids see only on TV or at other people's houses. They were psyched to the point of giddiness that this trip offered a whole summer of stuff I call junk.

I made music and videotapes to get us through the trip's longest, dullest parts. Music for me, videos for the kids. The van had an entertainment system. Adam successfully argued for bringing both the Nintendo and Playstation systems. I taped from CDs and the radio and ended up with eclectic mixes that had Tennessee Ernie Ford's "How Great Thou Art" segueing into Steven Tyler doing "Walk This Way." We were ready for stretches like the 13-hour Texas crossing. Classic rock n'roll peppered with touches of Lee Greenwood and Andrea Bocelli; hours of "Friends" reruns; two video controllers so Adam could beat his sister at Mario Kart; cases of Wal-Mart root beer.

Time to go.

# 2

## SETTING OUT: Massachusetts, Connecticut, New York, Pennsylvania

Yesterday we'd said goodbye to Mike. He had a business trip, so we'd stood at the kitchen door, hugging, and crying a little, trying to get through the farewell with as little hurt as possible. "I'll call you on the cellphone," I said a few times, already tapping into the value of this thing I'd resisted owning and hadn't yet used. Adam and Mike shook hands and exchanged masculine back pats.

Dana hugged her daddy tight. "Don't worry, Dane. I'll see you all in a month. It'll go by fast." Mike planned to meet us in Fort Bragg, California and travel with us for 10 days.

The premature goodbye made it easier to leave home. We only had to bear seeing our house disappear as we turned the first corner, instead of our dad and husband. About four miles from home we crossed the boundary marking our everyday lives' routine travel range. We picked up our first interstate. The journey began.

By the time we'd crossed Connecticut, New Paint was transformed. Somewhere around Hartford, the family car became a comfortable home, a secure haven, a dependable workhorse, a full member of the expedition. The kids settled in with their pillows and books and headphones. I eased into the rhythm of the road. And New Paint purred confidently westward, thrilled to be released from post office and grocery store runs. We were four travelers- three with legs, one with wheels.

I'll remember Fishkill, New York as the place where my mind grasped the magic and enormity of what we were doing. The pull of the road; the lure of unknown places; the freedom of being away. These gripped me as we filled our water bottles at the Fishkill rest area and gazed over the history-steeped Hudson River Valley falling away just beyond the endless line of truckers resting in their rigs.

Letters on the trucks and license plates told of vast stretches of highway leading to the places where these tired men lived when they weren't on the road: Tomah, Wisconsin; Lincoln, Nebraska; Texas; Louisiana; Minneapolis. Hard-working men delivering things Americans want and need, catching some sleep in the late afternoon on the side of the road in Fishkill, New York.

The Hamilton Fish Bridge carried us over the Hudson and into Pennsylvania, where the setting sun blazed orange as it nestled into the gray-green, hazy humps of the Allegheny foothills. Great tunnels blasted through mountains with names like Kittatinny and Tuscarora carried us into the state's core. We rolled through sooty Scranton and past

Wilkes-Barre, its trim three-story houses marching uphill from the great twin-spired brick church down in the town's center.

As we neared Hershey the next day, the sun played on the corrugated tin that sheathed white barns and silver silos. The silos were rocket ships waiting to blast from green fields. There was no shortage of places to pray in the farming hamlets that sat near Hershey. From Grantville, a tiny town of churches, to the East Hannover Mennonite Church, "All Welcome" signs told travelers there was always room in the pew for one more.

"Baby, you gotta wait in the line. That's what it's all about," sighed a mother to her I'm-too-cool-for-this daughter. They stood next to us in the Hershey Park ride line. I felt sorry for the woman, trying to carve out a halfway decent day with her kid, who was acting beastly. I'd have told her to wait in the car, made her pay me back the 35 bucks I'd spent on her ticket, and enjoyed the rides by myself.

We had fun in the lines. "Adam, those girls are checking you out," I whispered, as another long wait ate up more chunks of our Pennsylvania time. "Okay," he said, turning to cop a look at two sweet young things in "Angel" and "Princess" t-shirts who'd followed us from the Scrambler to the Twister.

"Okay" means "fine with me, that's good, I approve, thanks, I get it, cool, alright" – a positive reaction catchall phrase. At this babes-in-tiny-t-shirts moment, it probably also meant, "Maybe this trip won't be so bad…"

Once out of theme park heaven – or hell, depending on your viewpoint – we crossed the wide Susquehanna. A dozen hawks soared above us, floating between the high stone hills that hugged the road.

Our Donegal, Pennsylvania motel sat near the BP station - good for filling up, not good for Friday night sleeping. The music of a Donegal Friday night is the continuous screech of teenagers peeling out of the BP, sound systems at high bass and high volume, burning rubber down Route 31 to the Dairy Queen.

Even without the earsplitting coming of age ritual, I wouldn't have slept in Donegal. The chatty gentleman who checked in just before us ("On my way to Virginia to see the grandkids.") had nabbed the last non-smoking room ("The missus'll gag if I take smoking."). So, I took the hit for her, wishing I could put my nose on the nightstand until morning to get it away from the stink that started in the pillowcase, then permeated every ounce of polyester fiberfill. I resolved to never again rent a smoking room. We'd keep driving, or sleep in the van, maybe in a Wal-Mart parking lot.

Morning brought sweet silence, fresh air and Fallingwater. The kids knew the Guggenheim and knew Frank Lloyd Wright's stuff was funky, but they gave me the "We're gonna tour a house?" lament anyway. Until they saw it. We followed our guide, Justin, into all the cantilevered corners of the cement and steel aerie, and imagined what it must have been like to be Lillian Kaufman or her two Edgars and live in a place that belonged, in every sense save ownership, to the platform-shoed egoist who built it.

We loved it, even the treehouse-like ticket pavilion with deep eco-friendly toilets that terrified one girl so much she burst from the stall shouting, "I can't go! It's too scary!"

Back in the van, as Dana told and retold the scary bathroom story, we laughed, at more than the story. Something good had just clicked into place, and we knew we were going to enjoy this trip - and each other. If we could have this much fun talking about toilets, and dishing on Frank Lloyd for getting mad at Lillian because she didn't like his dining room chairs, just imagine what great times lay ahead! An entire country's worth! We opened some bags and cans of junk food, cranked the tunes, and headed for West Virginia.

# 3

# INTO THE SOUTH: West Virginia, Kentucky, Tennessee

A little boy in a bright white barber's cape sat on a barstool on the front porch of a house a hundred feet from the Mason-Dixon Line. His mom cut his hair while she talked with neighbors and family sitting on the wooden steps and on the faded couches that lined the porch railing.

Route 381 delivered us to West Virginia. At Bobbie's Texaco in Beverly, our second Justin of the trip filled the tank while we counted the gaudy ceramic angels in the window and read about the Pistol Training Course for a Concealed Weapon Permit to be held in the conference room of the Courthouse Annex. The gas station had no end of things to look at and consider, including a parting billboard that declared, "Some People Get Lost in Thought Just Because It's Unfamiliar Territory."

Since Pennsylvania's undulating Laurel Highlands, New Paint had been working hard, cresting hills and small mountains, then controlling herself nicely on the downhills, some of which were outfitted with serious Runaway Truck Ramps. I checked the rearview mirror frequently.

Between hills, we'd driven through the hearts of Pennsylvania towns made up of churches (one "Celebrating 228 years"), granges and gun clubs ("Turkey Shoot Every Sun. in Oct/Nov & Karaoke" – presumably not at the same time), and farmers' fields with tightly rolled wheels of hay sitting massive and yellow. Smithfield's centerpiece was the Mt. Moriah Baptist Church, beautiful brick and wood, festooned with scores of small

American flags that fluttered in the hot breeze and made you want to wave back.

Near Uniontown, New Paint narrowly missed a man climbing out of the woods by the road. He'd just nailed a handpainted "Gospel Sing" sign to a tree. More "Sing" signs in Fairchance and York. The sign-nailer had covered a lot of ground, fixing signs to miles of roadside trees. They were like a trail of breadcrumbs. A final sign pointed the way to the gathering place up Outcrop Road. We were tempted, but West Virginia lay just ahead, and its soft curves and green hills tempted us more.

West Virginia defined itself on entry as a non-stop mountain, so New Paint put on her game face and eased us up velvet heights and down into pristine valleys threaded with rushing rivers.

A biker rally was in full throttle somewhere near Marlinton. Bikers had claimed a hundred miles of rooms and tent sites, so Appalachia turned into one long quest for beds. We passed on an available space in the Tygart Valley Campground on account of two pigs snuffling around in the dirt.

And, we drove the six miles back down the mountain from a state campground because the forest it sat in seemed to be a hangout for pickups full of men and boys in camouflage t-shirts. "There don't seem to be any women or families up here," I said, preparing my two tired companions for the news that we wouldn't be stopping here, either. Intuition is a traveler's best friend, and, when it speaks, I listen. I maneuvered a 12-point turn and headed back down the dirt road, dueling banjos playing in my head.

"Mom, why aren't we staying up here?" asked Dana.

"Because it doesn't feel right."

"Okay," said two voices in unison from New Paint's rear.

Adam and Dana know about traveler's intuition, have seen it used before, and had no more questions about why we weren't pitching camp up here in the woods. Headphones went back in ears, Oreos got opened, and on we went.

We could have stayed at the Marlinton Motor Inn. The gracious lady at the front desk had one room left, "right next to where they're havin' the bonfire and karaoke tonight, if you don't mind that..." It was the last night of the biker fest, and people were primed to party. For a terrifying second or two, I let my brain play with the image of the kids and me locked in a motel room surrounded by a mob of inebriated bikers belting out karaoke around a bonfire. We moved on.

Marlinton's innkeepers made a valiant collective attempt to put a roof over our heads. The bonfire lady put in a call to the Graham Motel. No answer. At River Place, full to its highly varnished rafters, Dottie got the Graham on the phone. Booked solid. So, Dottie sent us up the hill to the Jericho. Owner Alice was rocking on her front porch, to which she'd affixed a "No Vacancy" sign in small, polite letters. She invited us in and put me on the phone with Jeannie at the Carriage House. Jeannie had an $85 attic suite, but she was east, near Virginia, and I couldn't spare the detour's extra miles. Jeannie told me to come back when we had more time. We left Marlinton without a room, but with fond memories of good people.

Stone ledges overhung the sweet mountain road that twisted and climbed toward Lewisburg. We'd bought subs in Marlinton. The kids laid New Paint's middle seat down like a table and sat in the rear, watching "My Wife and Kids" reruns. We had food, the kids were content, and I was ready to drive all night.

We found a room at a Lewisburg motel where the Hindu managers burned incense at the lobby altar and sat, palms upturned, mouthing prayers on the couch. Taped in the motel's front window were an American flag urging us to "Travel Proud" and a flyer offering a $10,000 reward for information leading to the arrest of the person who started a fire that took the life of a Roncaverte man.

Somewhere near Pearl Buck's birthplace, stately and pillared and neighbor to several miniature horse farms, we called Mike. "Hi daddy! There are lots of horses in West Virginia!" Dana saw West Virginia as the only thing that stood between her and Kentucky horse country, the holy grail of her American road trip. Back in Pennsylvania, she'd started asking, "Are we near Kentucky?" Now we were, and visions of horses danced through her head.

West Virginia is a beauty contest between rushing rivers and green mountains. It is a place that pulls you outdoors, clears your mind, and settles your soul. Adam and Dana had never camped, and West Virginia was the place to fix that.

One late afternoon, at New River Gorge, we scouted a site at a small campground on a creek, and checked ourselves in via the honor system. This was grand adventure for the kids, and they took off down the dirt roads and through the woods to scope out the portable johns and water pumps, the shower building, and the communal enamel dishwashing sink. They filled the water jugs, gathered firewood, and arranged our folding chairs and little plastic tables. They unpacked exciting gear like flashlights and the Coleman lamp, and spread clothes and sleeping bags to claim their spots inside the three-man tent.

Brian, the campground owner, came by on his golf cart to welcome us and collect our fee. He took Adam on a spin down to the outhouse to replace toilet paper. His tree-climbing dog Loca was busy in the woods, rushing at terrified squirrels. She was quite a sight, running crazed up the vertical trunks, then flipping backward and landing in the dirt. Loca was nuts, and the squirrels were traumatized. They hadn't figured out that the tree would peel her off and send her plummeting, just in time, every time.

As the crisp West Virginia dusk fell, we settled into our outdoor home. The evening was special. Wireless neophyte, I was awed by the ability to talk to Mike on a phone while standing in a remote Appalachian forest. (I'd already called him that day, from the mouth of a coal mine.) Adam was chief cook and fire tender, and the meal of canned corn and beef stew he heated up was a culinary tour de force. It was, then and there in the cool woods, the best meal we'd ever had. As evening moved toward night, we sat in our little chairs and talked. "Imagine living at Fallingwater..." whispered Dana. We imagined, as fireflies blinked in the blackness, and campfire licks lit our faces. We imagined, to the sounds of woods and darkness and the distant lullaby hum of the big rigs out on Route 119.

We made our way through West Virginia, a place of beauty and brawn. I'd fallen in love with the Kanawha, a broad, heartland river, at once gentle and tough. It meandered alongside the Midland Trail, a coal route, which linked blue-collar towns like Alloy, Boomer, and Smithers, to Charleston. Three parallel lines - river, rails, road - told you these were places that worked hard for a living. Moss-green erector set bridges crossed the Kanawha, and we looked down onto black mountains of coal piled in barges tethered to riverside docks. The front steps of the London Church of Christ were carpeted with aqua Astroturf, and the Twin Falls Restaurant near Shrewsbury advertised "Good Down Home Cooking —West Virginia People Doing Business West Virginia Style."

The Chuck Yeager Bridge took us over the Kanawha into Charleston. Sunlight bounced off the capitol's great gold dome, and fine brick mansions sat on a high bluff above the river. We toured old Charleston's cobbled sections for a while and then, at a "Got Milk?" billboard of white-mustachioed Dixie Chicks, found I-64, which would lead, eventually, to horse country. I shot a big smile into the back seat from the rearview mirror: "OK, Dane. We're officially on our way to Kentucky."

A bridge over the Big Sandy River took us over the state line. Dusty, ochre ugliness. Kentucky wasn't supposed to be dry and beige. It was supposed to be rich and green. What was this brown limestone world, this claylike landscape of dirty yellow rock, this Daniel Boone Forest that didn't seem to have any trees? I made an emergency stop at the Ponderosa buffet in Morehead, so we could fill ourselves with comfort food and recover from the disappointment of learning that Kentucky – at least this part of it – was not very pretty.

Closer to Lexington, redemption. Hints of green and blue. Patches, then whole pastures, of rolling, perfect grass. Grass that nurtures champions. Mare and foal pairs in love and nuzzling, savoring their time together, sunlight on their withers. Horses so beautiful you wanted to cry. Elegance and long legs and strong backs and power bred for a purpose. This was Lexington.

Dana's dream became real, mile by white rail-fenced mile. The horses were pure majesty. I watched Adam watch Dana. I could see him decide to go with the flow and let his sister enjoy. I filled up. My daughter was in her place of a young lifetime, we were surrounded by equine beauty that took your breath away, and Adam was showing himself to be a true gentleman.

Our Lexington days were all horse. We made an eight-hour, 85-in-the-shade, no-square-inch-missed visit to Kentucky Horse Park. We went three times to Thoroughbred Park to leap among and sit atop the life-size bronze Derby contenders. We stalked a pair of Lexington cops and their chestnut mounts as they walked their Main Street beat. "The police even ride horses!" marveled Dana, as she added law enforcement to her mental list of jobs for horse lovers.

I don't think Dana slept much the night before our dawn pilgrimage to Keeneland Racecourse to watch the morning workouts. When I whispered in her ear at 5:30 that it was time to get up, her eyes shot open, and her face beamed. We dressed quietly so we wouldn't wake Adam, slipped out, and went downstairs for a quick breakfast before heading into the already hot Lexington pre-dawn. We were the first breakfast customers of the morning. As we passed the reception desk, I whispered to the clerk, "We're off to Keeneland." "Ahhhh," she whispered back, nodding at Dana with a knowing look, telepathy transmitted from one horse lover to another. "You'll love it." I looked at Dana, always beautiful, and, at this moment, the most excited, gorgeous little girl on the planet.

We traced a route around venerable Keeneland along parts of the Bluegrass Driving Tour, following Rice and Van Meter and Versailles ("We say 'ver-SALES', not fancy like the one in France," the night desk clerk had told me when I'd come down to ask the best route from the hotel to Keeneland.). Dana could have spent hours on these roads, each a thin, gray ribbon along which lay some of Lexington's most storied horse farms. The pastures were lush green carpet, the architecture distinctive and utterly beautiful. Crisp lines, fresh paint, rich trim. Pristine clapboards and elegant cupolas, graceful weathervanes. Dana has an encyclopedic knowledge of everything equine and, from her reading, was more familiar with these farms than I, and her excitement as we read their names – John Ward, Drumkenny, Broodmare, Manchester, Fares - traveled like an electrical current, stirring in me a deep contentment. We pulled over by a white rail fence on a slight rise in Rice Boulevard and looked out over the pastures spreading before us, hints of blue visible in the rich grass as it waited in the low, early light for the new day to burn off the night's dew and mist.

On Van Meter, the red trim on the outbuildings of a vast farm betrayed it as Calumet, and, as we neared its fences, from a stand of tall trees that graced a velvety grass hillock, came a line of grooms, all Latino, each man leading a stunning thoroughbred on a rope. The line of small, silent men and sinewy horses flowed down the hillock toward us, then turned left and continued, parallel to the fence and the road we watched from, keeping under the shade of the trees, then turned left again, gently ambling back up the rise toward Calumet's stables.

At Keeneland, we stood at the rail of the fabled oval, the only spectators, and watched trainers lead horses from the misty rows of silvery stables and onto the track. Light, lean, blue-jeaned trainers, one with dreadlocks flying from under his helmet, put pounding, sweating thoroughbreds through their paces. The trainers wore helmets, and most wore chest pads. They carried crops, which they weren't shy about using. Some stood, others crouched. Some made their horses step sideways. The men and animals took the track's bends and straightaways at breakneck speeds. Old Joe, tall and gaunt and wrinkled, in jeans and western shirt and a helmet with a pom-pom on top, sat astride his horse, Frog. They sat at the track rail, inside and on the course, ready to go after runaways. That was their job. Joe's eyes were peeled, and he was ready to ride Frog to the rescue of any trainer whose trainee decided he'd rather be somewhere else.

A good number of the riders took note of Dana. A little girl with a beautiful brown ponytail who'd risen before the sun to stand at the rail. Like this morning's desk clerk, they recognized her as a kindred spirit. They smiled, waved, and slowed down when they passed so she could look longer at their horses. Dana had brought her little plastic camera, and some of the trainers posed for pictures.

One trainer with a gentle face and shining eyes assembled himself and three others into a parade formation. They passed us, four abreast, at a slow, regal posting trot, like palace guard presenting the colors before the queen, each rider smiling down at Dana. I thanked them with my eyes. That they took note and took time turned this special morning into magic. These were busy men with hard work to do. Some were watched by the horse owners who paid them, and they weren't paid to be nice to little girls. But they were, and I'll always remember them with fondness.

Before we left Keeneland, as the first brush of hot, higher-than-horizon sun kissed the bluegrass, we ventured into the great grandstand and sat awhile in Mr. George Goodman's personalized box, imagining what it would be like to settle in here in the cool shade on a sunny race day to watch the horses and the other racegoers.

Adam had slept until we turned the key back in the door. "Breakfast is about to close. You'd better get down there, bud." On this trip, I left no hotel amenity unturned, amassing a sack full of little soaps, and bottles of shampoo that I used to wash our clothes in the sink or bathtub. And, I encouraged the eating of any available free food. I looked for the magic words "Free Continental Breakfast" on motel signs. Sometimes we hit pay dirt, finding a motel that also hosted a "manager's happy hour." This meant free dinner, because, next to the beer and wine and soda, the manager usually laid out cheese and crackers and a big tray of crudité. The kids drew the line at raw cauliflower and broccoli, but tucked into the celery, carrots and cherry tomatoes, huge dollops of dip on the side. Sometimes pay dirt turned to mother lode, with a spread that included things like tacos and little egg rolls.

Through careful husbandry of free motel fare and a manager's cocktail hour here and there, we were occasionally able to patch together a string of five free meals in a row: free breakfast at Motel 1; free lunch of apples, bagels and peanut butter (cream cheese for Dana) spirited from Motel 1 breakfast spread; free dinner from Motel 2 happy hour; free breakfast at Motel 2; free lunch spirited from Motel 2 breakfast spread.

By meal number six, we were ready for a restaurant, and we always voted unanimously on type: Mexican. (Curiously, we'd eat our worst Mexican food in Texas and our best in North Dakota.)

Dana and I accompanied Adam down to the breakfast bar. "So, how was it?" he asked, of our visit to Keeneland. He asked Dana, directly. I wanted to hug him over his plate of biscuits and gravy. As she wove a tale of the magic kingdom of Keeneland, Adam listened and chewed. While it was clear he thought Keeneland sounded cool – he said, "Okay" a few times as Dana talked – I knew he didn't feel he'd missed anything. Dana preferred horses, he preferred sleep. He was content they'd both gotten what they most wanted from the morning.

That night, while I worked on my first installment for the newspaper, Dana was writing her own story, "Horse Capital of the World." It begins: "In the heart of Lexington, Kentucky, lies a beauty like no other..."

Before we left Kentucky, Scotty, the hotel's maintenance man, cleaned New Paint and prepared her for takeoff. He wanted to release the green machine from the shroud of Allegheny and Appalachia dust that covered her before we headed grill-first into the rest of our adventure. As part of his job involves cleaning things and keeping them neat and in order, I think our dirt had been bothering him for days. He stopped me in the parking lot one afternoon.

"You could use a car wash."

"We sure could."

"You want me to go over it with this hose?"

"That'd be lovely."

"Okay. I just needed your permission."

We'd met Scotty on our first day. When we told him what we were up to, he said, "I've wanted to do that all my life." He considered our trip aloud: how big it was; how filled it would be with interesting people and places; how long we'd be gone; that we'd come this far already; that these two young kids were living a

20

dream that many people had; that he envied his retired brother who spent his days driving around the country in his RV; that New Orleans was "not much of anything, but you gotta go."

He sought us out and spent whatever time he could away from hoses and pipes and bosses to talk about our crossing America. We were in the pool one morning, kids diving and splashing, I trying to execute a meaningful pool-running workout, when Scotty spied us and pulled a beach chair close to the pool's edge to talk about America and all there was to see.  I had to make my running laps excruciatingly small so I could stay within earshot and offer decent conversation.

When he talked, he was reflective, pensive. He made us feel our trip into the healing country was important.  He seemed proud of us, and I realized that that mattered to me. We'd meet many people like Scotty. That summer, the simple act of one family's trip across the nation was enough to connect Americans in a certain, knowing bond. We were there, on the road, out in the nation, terrorism-be-damned, we're going to see it and drink it in and absorb it and love it and experience the wonder of it because it's ours and you can't knock it down or take it away.  I realized that people we met were cheering us on and that we represented them. Perhaps they couldn't make the trip themselves, but we could make it for them, touching the county's corners and middles, confirming that things were and would be alright. We - Adam, Dana, New Paint and I- were a cord, a thread. We had the capacity to sew patches of the vast American quilt together simply by threading our way through it and talking to people we met. These revelations were gifts from Scotty.

We left Lexington at 7 a.m. in light, gray rain. Scotty was in the parking lot. He stood and waved. "So! You're on the road already! Off to see the world!"  He watched us leave until we were out of sight.

Before we got into New Paint, gleaming from her wash, I'd taken Adam aside. "You let your sister have the experience she came for. I'm proud of you."

A little nod, then, "Okay."

As we headed for Tennessee, we peered down four-digit roads like 1517 and 1462. Two Amish boys in their horse buggy pulled out of the Sonora Plaza Truck Stop, where back road Kentucky meets I-65.

We had a pit stop to make. In Bowling Green, across from the GM plant, sits the white snail-shaped Corvette Museum, an Adam must-see. Immediately off the exit ramp, things got weird. Had we been dropped in an automobile version of *The Stepford Wives*? Every other car in Bowling Green was a Corvette. "Look at all the Vettes parked at that motel!" "All the cars at that drive-thru window are Corvettes!" We stopped at a red light. Every car facing us, stopped and waiting across the intersection, was a Corvette. I looked to my right. The guy stopped beside us sat in a Corvette.

At the museum, two parking lots. By this point, New Paint was one of my heroes. But, with a flick of his wrist, the parking lot attendant declared her a second-class car and sent us to the nearly vacant "non-Corvette parking lot." A Corvette owners convention had brought thousands of Vettes, from vintage to showroom fresh, to Bowling Green. And all of them, except the ones still back in town at the red light or the fast food joint or the motels, were parked in the special, Corvettes-only parking lot, making it at least as interesting as the museum.

Adam wandered the museum in reverent silence. When he got behind the wheel of the one Corvette you could sit in, I had to rub my eyes to change him back into a 13-year-old boy. For an instant, I saw a confident, independent young man. I gave thanks for this trip and this time I'd been given to spend with him before he outgrew me.

The road from Kentucky led to my friend Rhonda's house, outside Nashville. We've known each other since we were 14, when I was in love with her cousin Rick. After he broke my heart, we stayed friends. Rhonda was the only person I'd made plans to visit.

Like many of their neighbors, Rhonda and husband Charlie came to Nashville to follow work. While on a 6 a.m. power walk through her development, once a vast farm, I watched people transplanted from Michigan and the northeast drive off to jobs at Dell Computer or the car plants at Spring Hill and Smyrna. As I circumnavigated the tidy neighborhood, I noticed what looked like "For Sale" signs planted on some of the front lawns. When I got close enough to read them, I learned that "The 10 Commandments Are Supported Here" and "Ye Must Be Born Again."

Rhonda and Charlie have adapted to their new culture. They'll always be Yankees, but their kids were born in the South. Erin and Paul go to Christian school, and their summer reading list included the Bible.

Our kids played together in the cul-de-sac, while Rhonda, Charlie and I drank beers on the front porch. Charlie's a traveler. Real travelers know geography, even of places they haven't been to yet. I described our route, and Charlie sat back and smiled, visualizing the Stonehenge of old Cadillacs sticking up in Amarillo, the jagged reaches of the Sawtooth, the forested shores of Lake Huron. This is a guy who, years ago, got in a car with a few buddies and drove from Boston to Yellowknife, just to see what a place called Yellowknife looked like. They spent a few hours there and drove home. I understood completely.

Rhonda's house had been a psychological safety net. It was a familiar destination.    A place where we'd been expected. Somewhere with people who cared about us.    A chance to stretch out and hang around a house with a yard and lots of rooms and a washing machine and a kitchen with food. A visit with friends.    A point from which I could turn around and go home if something wasn't right about this trip and still feel the venture had been worthwhile.

We left Rhonda's driveway and left the safety net behind.    We were on our own, for the next 10,000 miles.    We drove into America, and it embraced us.

## 4

# *FROM MEMPHIS TO THE DELTA: Mississippi, Louisiana*

As part of its "Hour of Classical Music," Memphis public radio played the Kansas City Chorale singing "Johnny I Hardly Knew Ye," an Irish war lament whose haunting melody echoes the Civil War song, "When Johnny Comes Marching Home." The doleful notes, the chants of "drums and guns and drums and guns," and the long, hushed "hurroos" hung in the air like spirits unable to sleep.

Since Tennessee, the war whose ghosts walked the landscape had changed. Farther north, we'd passed fieldstone taverns where the Continental Army had planned attacks on redcoats. Now, we passed silent fields where hundreds or thousands of boys in gray and blue died.

The weight of war felt heavier in the south than I feel it up north. Back home, buildings and monuments of the Revolution are the stuff of school field trips to clapboard places like Paul Revere's house. Its fighters are valiant figures with rousing collective names- Sons of Liberty, Founding Fathers, Green Mountain Boys. But those men were over two hundred years away from us, known through writings and artists' renderings. I thought of them as icons, not as somebody's son, brother, father or friend.

Here, it was closer, more intimate. The boys who lie under this grass were not so far in time from us. There were photographs to show who they really were. We could study their eyes and hands and the buttons on their shirts. They were men and boys somebody loved and cried for. When we passed the sign for Shiloh, Adam and I exchanged a glance. Shiloh. The word had a powerful sadness. We had left behind places where Americans created the nation and now looked on places where they almost took it apart. The hush of these southern knolls and grasses intensified the ability to imagine the death played out here. As if it happened yesterday. I'd never felt so palpably connected to war.

Yet, from what I'd seen since we left Boston, love of the country we became bridged any regional divide. From Massachusetts to Tennessee, the Stars and Stripes adorned barnsides, billboards, truck panels, car windows. Messages of encouragement and patriotic optimism hung from churches, restaurants, beauty parlors, used car dealerships. Only one flag flew over America that summer, and one message of unity. The country was declaring that, while it was needed and for as long as it was needed, all its parts would stay welded into a galvanized whole. Throughout our journey, the declaration rang clear. It was an invisible tensile thread stretching into every corner of the country, sewing it together.

I-40 now had a name as well as a number: The Music Highway. A stretch named for Carl Perkins. The Johnny Cash Rest Area, where a family from New Jersey decamped from a huge, black SUV, mom on one cellphone, dad on another.

We entered Memphis on Sam Cooper Boulevard, where a billboard urged people to "Rollerskate For Health." Union Avenue's parade of huge churches – Methodist, Presbyterian, Baptist, Catholic – led through downtown to the Mississippi.

We crossed the river's pedestrian bridge to Mud Island and its scale model of the river system. The kids splashed downriver all the way to Memphis from Cairo, Illinois. We stood on Old Man River's real bank and tried to find a place where Adam could cast his line into the water. Before we left home, he'd bought himself a collapsible rod and a stocked tackle box and was looking forward to a little fishing here and there. And here was the Mississippi. I offered an Adam-Huck simile, got a teenager look, and let fly my happiness anyway. I was standing in the sun on the banks of America's greatest river with my barefoot kids, one smiling wide and happy, one with rod in hand.

We watched the world's luckiest ducks wrap up a day of lolling in the Peabody Hotel's lobby fountain. Ushered by a bellman, the ducks climbed out of the fountain on a tiny ladder and waddled on a red carpet to the elevator that whisked them to their penthouse. Spectators clutched five-dollar bar drinks and bags of duck souvenirs from the gift shop.

At the Rum Boogie Café on Beale Street, I held the cellphone up to the band so Mike could hear some blues. The music was wonderful, but I was more excited by my still novel ability to make a phone call from the middle of a Memphis dance floor.

We left Beale about 7:30 p.m., just as dusk dropped and seriously armed and muscled cops in groups of four began to appear. On the riverbank, people filed up the gangway for the 8 p.m. cruise on the *Mississippi Queen*. The night and the river were red and purple, and the soft green lights on the steel bridge that held the Arkansas state line in its middle glowed like mints.

Before we left Memphis early the next morning, we stood in front of the Lorraine Motel. A white wreath hangs on a blue metal railing, marking the second-floor room where Martin Luther King died. I'd hoped to see Jacqueline Smith, the protestor who's camped for years across from the Lorraine and who lived in it before it became the National Civil Rights Museum. All her stuff was there on the corner. Her boxes and cardboard and signs. I half-wanted to stick around and meet her. I wanted to hear her story. I wanted to hear her tell how money spent on the museum could do more civil right by improving living conditions for Memphis' black poor. But we had miles to cover, and Smith was still in bed somewhere, probably on a friend's couch. We left

Memphis as the sun rose, rays bouncing off a riverbank jogger puffing along in something that looked like a tin foil spacesuit.

Shortly after a quick stop at the graffiti wall outside Graceland, where I took a picture of Roop and his father from California and mentioned, perhaps unwisely, that we weren't real Elvis fans, we entered Mississippi and rode the sterile interstate all the way to Vicksburg. We drove the powerfully haunted battlefield road and looked down sobering rows of endless gravestones in the cemetery.

"Boiled and Green Peanuts." "Home Grown Peaches." "Fresh Catfish and Pantrout." "Crawfish Boiled or Live." Route 61 rode us all the way through Port Gibson, too beautiful for Grant to burn, to a small piece of a long stretch of road I've wanted to ride since I was a kid. The Natchez Trace. Trace. Not road or highway, but trace. A whisper of something fleeting and gone past.

We rode 40 miles on the Trace to its terminus at Natchez. Deep green New Paint blended into the primal moss forest, dark and rich. Speed limit on the Trace is 50, "but nobody does," according to the lady in the Port Gibson tourist office. We did that and less, wanting to feel the soul and pace of the Indians and trappers whose lifeline this old road used to be.

We met National Park Service ranger Daniel Kimes, who'd just been stationed at Emerald Mound, a 700-year-old ceremonial mound built by ancestors of the Choctaw. I'd targeted Emerald Mound as consolation for missing Cahokia. Like other very old American places, scattered and sometimes hard to find, this sacred, grass-covered earthwork reminds us we're a new land in an old land. As its builders did centuries before us, we climbed the green, conical hill, surveyed the encircling forest, and thought about the land.

"I grew up on the Trace," said Kimes. "This is a dream come true for me." He'd be going up to Philly or Boston or D.C. in August for a stint watching the historic sites, Park Service practice since September 11, but he was savoring his time at Emerald Mound, deep in the ancient woods of the Trace.

When we got to Natchez, we sized it up as a good place to fish, and we drove to Bailey Park early one morning so Adam could spend some quality river time before the day's high heat and humidity set in. He looked under the seat for his rod and tackle box. "Where are they, mom? I gave them to you to hold."

So he did, back in Vicksburg, where I'd laid them down to take a picture. I felt worse than bad. Adam had been looking forward to this. Up in town, there was a K-Mart next to the Natchez Market, where the day before we'd spent a few fun minutes watching red plastic shopping carts roll through the downhill-sloping parking lot and bump into shoppers' cars. I told Adam I'd replace his equipment as soon as K-Mart opened. But that was over an hour away, and I had ruined this perfect fishing morning. Adam was decent about not rubbing it in, but did utilize his keen eye for opportunity: "Since I'm so devastated, can I have a root beer for breakfast?"

Two men in a pickup backed down the cement boat ramp pushing a Bass Tracker. "How you doin' today?" asked the driver.

I pointed at Adam, sucking down his 7 a.m. root beer. "Well, right now we're trying to get over the fact that mom left his fishing rod in a park back in Vicksburg."

John and Mac immediately became everything good about Mississippi that we needed to know. Our chance meeting meant they couldn't solve the rod problem ("If I'd a known these kids was gonna be here, we'd a brought some rods – Mac's got about ten," sighed John), but they found other ways to show the kids a fine Mississippi River time.

They hoisted Adam and Dana into the bass boat and opened coolers holding yesterday's catch. Three catfish, a whiskered one and two flatheads, each about six pounds, sat on ice. They looked huge to me, but Mac dismissed them as small, unprofitable fry he hoped he'd be able to sell. "The best eatin' catfish are about eight to nine pounds." Size matters in catfish. "Caught a 76-pounder once. Too big. Bad eatin'. Too much fat. Nobody'd buy it."

Mac told of the "evidence" of a 110-pounder capable of turning the who-eats-whom tables. "River's got stories." He pointed to a spot in the river. "Right out there. Eat a man whole." As Adam listened to the fish tales, I imagined him wanting to get to K-Mart as soon as possible to retool so he could reel in one of these leviathans. He probably also fantasized that I'd empty the Thule and fill it with ice, so we could haul the thing around for a while.

Mac did most of the talking while John got ready to launch. He was going to cross to Vidalia on the Louisiana side to check some catfish lines he'd sunk near a spot where a new hotel was going up. He offered to take us along for the ride. It was tempting to go out on the Father of Waters and watch a Natchez fisherman at work.

But I couldn't. While intuition sounded the all clear, I needed to err on the side of too much caution when it came to decisions about safety or vulnerability. Keeping my guard up wasn't something I could compromise on this trip, even if it meant missing some experiences. I had a fitting, but truthful excuse.

"Thank you, but I'm afraid of the water." Mac, either sharp, sympathetic, or both, said he understood my fear. "So's John's girlfriend. She won't get in the boat." Then he added, "This river's taken a lot of my friends."

But he loved it. "I been on every inch of her. I've camped on all these sandbars, me and my wife. We got a generator and TV."

The signature steel bridge that connects Natchez with Vidalia began to shimmer with heat as the sun assumed its position over the Mississippi. Mac and John told us that about four years back, the water level was so low you could stand on the bridge and look down on a pile of cars and trucks, dumped into the river when a barge hit the bridge in 1945.

By now, John had an overdue date with some catfish lines, and K-Mart was open and ready to sell us new fishing gear. We shook hands. John looked at Adam. "Take care of your mama."

We felt happy as we drove away. The whole day and the whole country were ahead, and everything we'd left behind was good. "Just think, Adam. Some kid in Vicksburg is catching catfish right now." Adam smiled. "Yeah, that's what I was thinking."

We entered Louisiana at West Feliciana Parish. Elegant egrets sunned on broad sandbars in the wide, muddy Homochitto River. "Bienvenue en Louisiane" said the sign on Route 61. In St. Francisville, gas stations sold hot boiled crawfish, and the Feliciana Super-Valu sold them live for 69 cents a pound.

Sun-bleached shells, dredged from the Mississippi years ago and used as fill, covered the ground at the Westerfield family plot in the old Mount Carmel Cemetery. Three stone angels guarded the graves, and a piece of a Kipling poem hinted at the family's faith and good humor:

"When Earth's last picture is painted and the tubes are
twisted and dried
When the oldest colours have faded, and the youngest
critic has died,
We shall rest, and, faith, we shall need it –
lie down for an aeon or two,
Till the Master of All Good Workmen shall
put us to work anew."

Down by the St. Francisville ferry landing, Adam cast his K-Mart rod into the Mississippi and sank within seconds in riverbank mud that encased his sneakers and covered his calves. Had he stood there longer, he might have disappeared entirely. Even this didn't get a rise out of the guy selling Emily's Pralines to the line of cars waiting to board the ferry to New Roads. I'd tried talking to him as he waited under an umbrella between ferry line-ups, keeping the pralines in a cooler until there were enough cars to warrant loading up his little red wagon and walking down the line, but I got nothing, and gave up.

But our mud removal operation entertained the waiting drivers. We were parked where all could see, under a hulking pile of rusted cranes. I lifted New Paint's tailgate, revealing our stacked plastic box system, which had been wowing and amusing people since Pennsylvania. I also revealed the morning's laundry, drying atop the boxes. We had everybody's attention. People ate pralines and laughed while we cleaned mud gobs from Adam's shoes and feet and legs with plastic bags and baby wipes. I used all the water in our bottles and jugs, as the river water behind us was, well, the same mud we were trying to get rid of. By the time the ferry pulled up and disgorged people from the New Roads side, and our audience started to roll, we'd removed enough to let Adam and his shoes back into the van. But there was so much mud, I'd still be finding dried bits of it six weeks later in Cleveland.

We crossed the Mississippi at Baton Rouge, after a quick elevator ride up to the state capitol's 27th floor observation deck, from where the wide, brown, hard-working river spread massive beneath us as far as the eye could see. Two Japanese girls tapped my arm, pointed at the monster river, and said, in high-octave unison, "Excuse. Eez Meeseeseepee?" I took a second to recover from the astonishing question before confirming their suspicions. I pictured them traveling to northern Arizona, standing on the rim of a mind-blowing, multi-hued, mile-deep chasm that spread forever and ever, and asking the guy next to them if it was the Grand Canyon.

New Paint meandered toward New Orleans on small roads dominated by oil and petrochemical plants and punctuated by sleepy towns, churches, cemeteries, antebellum plantations and sugar cane fields. Being Sunday, Pinnacle Polymers and Dupont Elastomers were quiet, but churches were open all day for business. We passed one in Ascension Parish about 3 p.m., and members of the congregation, dressed to the nines, were gathered in the parking lot, chatting and socializing. The same at Mt. Calvary Church, where the men wore pressed dress pants and crisp snow white long-sleeved shirts, buttoned up proper even in the stifling heat and humidity. The women's dresses were jubilant statements in red and orange. The church sat near Pecan Street and looked directly onto the massive levee that hid and held back the Mississippi just beyond. You knew the river was there when a barge or tanker passed, showing only its top as it slid by.

A storm brewed as we entered the Big Easy on the concrete bridge that crosses Lake Pontchartrain. The black cloud that swallowed us, and the ugly swamp and decrepit railroad bridge running next to us made Adam whisper, "VOODOO!" Then, "I'm gonna try it." He asked me if it works. I said I hoped not, and asked, "Who ya gonna do voodoo to? It better not be me." The first thing he bought in New Orleans was a voodoo kit. The next day, when Dana's $160 in trip money, saved up over nine months, went missing from our hotel room, Adam told us one of the sticks he'd played around with in his voodoo kit had read, "You will lose a lot of money." We didn't see much more of the voodoo kit.

New Orleans is a steamy ethnic gumbo, equal parts rough and refined. An hour after we discovered Dana's money had been stolen, a store manager gave us free pralines because the cashier had charged us too much sales tax. Bawdy Mardi Gras beads hung from wizened branches of ancient trees, from elegant railings, from the handlebars of locked bicycles.

We called Mike from the Acme Oyster House in the Quarter to tell him what we were eating. Dana gave the report: "Hi Daddy, it's us. We're in New Orleans. Mommy is eating gumbo poopa, Adam has a po'boy, and I'm eating hush puppies."

The stall door in Acme's ladies' room advertised a product I'd never heard of – one that must sell well here. A poster touted Alka-Seltzer's MORNING RELIEF: "Fast Hangover Relief. TONIGHT You're Feeling Goooood. TOMORROW Feel Better Than You Should." Necessary equipment in the Quarter, where even quiet, polyestered couples walk around with cups of beer and tropically flavored alcohol in long neon-pink glasses, filled and refilled at "To-Go" bars.

Acme's oyster shucker was at work behind the bar as we read the Wall of Fame.

"Those the champion oyster eaters?" I asked.

"Those're the fools."

The shucker told me that the name of the new Leader of the House hadn't been put up yet. "Jes' las' week a guy et 41 dozen.

He's goin' on the Wall. An' you know what he et after that? Sof'
shell crab. Raw."

The new champ's name would join the likes of Bill Poole
from Berkley Heights, NJ, who downed 32 dozen while watching
Super Bowl XXIV in 1990, and Edna-Sara Lodin who carried
back to Stockholm well-earned tales of ingesting 16 dozen
Louisiana oysters on May 29, 2000. Way to go, Edna.

We fell in love with the Quarter and returned many times,
leaving the late evening and nighttime hours for revelers. We
enjoyed early morning and late afternoon walks down Chartres
and Decatur, watching the play of sunlight on bougainvillea
hanging from the doorways and gleaming iron balconies. Down
Royal and Iberville to take in the sherbet-colored facades and long
hunter green shutters that hid windows that met the pavement.
Down Bourbon and into Jackson Square to see the characters and
watch the palm and tarot readers and hear zydeco and Cajun
music spill onto the sidewalk from air-conditioned souvenir shops.
I pointed out the "horse carriages" lined up to take tourists
around and was duly educated on the differences between horses
and mules. Dana was amused I could mistake one for the other.
Even after the thorough equine identification lesson, it remained
tricky nuance to me. I was glad there wasn't a test.

For a genteel view of the city, we rode the Garden District's
St. Charles streetcar to the end and back. We got a slow, rolling
narration of the sights - wedding cake mansions, beautifully
painted shotgun houses, shady Audubon Park, the venerable side-
by-side campuses of Tulane and Loyola - from a funky little lady
who'd ridden the trolley down to Harrah's on the river, where
she'd played the nickel slots. She'd spent 15 cents and won 10
dollars. "I'm rich!" she laughed.

Leaving New Orleans, we drove the eerie gauntlet of Metairie
Cemetery's above- ground tombs, which line both sides of the
highway. An endless sea of bright white, cross-topped houses for
the dead.

35

We headed deeper into Acadiana. The Ragin' Cajun kept us entertained on 100.3 FM, with zydeco and accordions and lots of talk about fish rodeos. Prizes for the biggest redfish, lemon fish, seacat, speck, and sheephead. We crossed the Bayou Des Allemands and entered LaFourche Parish on a straight road where every yard held a boat, including an ark-in-progress with a sign that read, "That's a big boat PAW PAW." 100.3 spun more accordion-rich Cajun tunes celebrating "vivant sur les bayous Louisianes" and "la vie acadienne."

We were looking for a place to get into the swamp and see some gators. Adam found it. Munson's Swamp Tours sat seven miles off the highway in a cane field in Schriever. We had three hours before the next tour, so we took Bill Munson's advice on how to fill them, eating salisbury steak and mashed potatoes and catfish po'boys at Wilson's Kountry Korner, and heading down Route 309 to sightsee. "It's scenic," Bill had said. Eerie black cypress knees poked out of the duckweed-covered swamp on both sides of the thin road. A truck pulling a bass boat appeared ahead of us. "Follow that boat," urged Adam. His fishing rod was in his lap, ready to go. At Chacahoula, we passed the Silverado Lounge, where the band Way Down South was scheduled to play. We'd heard about the band from Otis, who'd called in to 100.3 to talk to the Ragin' Cajun.

Adam threw his line into a stinking canal near Leighton and got a few good pulls. Carrion eaters were nibbling the eyeballs from scores of bloated, severed fish heads that floated around the dock, so Dana and I told Adam to hurry it up. This was no idyllic Natchez scene.

Back at Munson's, we boarded a small pontoon with three passengers from California, also going cross-country. Their van was fitted out a lot like New Paint, and we peeked in each others' vehicles looking for improvement ideas for our own rolling homes. We envied their bigger interior space, and they envied our entertainment system and stacking boxes.

We made our way into the bayou with Joey, who'd been a Munson's guide for 12 years, and Ashley, who drove the boat. When I'd paid Bill Munson earlier, he assured me we'd picked the right tour and that we'd get more than "just a boat ride." He explained his swamp is private, with nothing to scare off the wildlife.

Bill and Deb Munson lease their bayou routes, once natural, but straightened when men came in to harvest cypress, from the Cox family, owners of the 3,600-acre Bull Run sugar cane plantation.

Rice grows north, but here near Houma, it's cane, processed at Raceland and Thibodaux plants. Joey knew everything about this watery land, its people, problems and pleasures. And he knew everything about alligators. Our little group, adults and kids alike, had a grand time out on the fecund, tree-draped bayou.

Joey and Ashley dangled raw chicken and hamburger buns over the pontoon's sides, an edible siren call to streams of gators that sliced through the brown water toward the boat. They came from all directions. They came three and four in a row, like an armada. Sometimes several swarmed the boat at once, jumping out of the water to snatch the chicken, swallowing it as they disappeared, then lurking for more.

This bayou was part of the Atchafalaya Basin, created by the Mississippi's natural course. John from California commented that the Mississippi would like to return to its true path, but man can't let it because "New Orleans'd be under water." Ashley grunted. "We don't need Nawlins. Nawlins is a big pain."

The raccoons on the banks kept two eyes open for the gators that lived to lunge out of the water and eat them. Joey pointed out a raccoon bridge – a giant cypress arched over the bayou and worn smooth from sliding raccoons. A baby raccoon house up in a tree kept orphans safe until they were grown, then released. Joey kept a baby at home. "Got 'im pretty much trained. He sucks his own bottle."

John and Adam asked Joey all the horrible black bayou what-if questions they could think of. Joey answered like a true Cajun.

"Is there quicksand?"

"There's slush. It'll fill in right over you."

"What if the boat starts to sink?"

"Git to the bank and climb a tree. That'd be your only chance."

"Anything else dangerous besides gators?"

"I'd rather wrastle an alligator than mess with the snakes."

"Lost anybody on the tour?"

"Don't keep track. It's bad for da business."


On the 4$^{th}$ of July, we found ourselves at Avery Island, home of McIlhenny's Tabasco Sauce factory. Being a holiday, the factory was closed, and the workers had a day off to crab. We hung at the dock outside McIlhenny's with 2-year old Trey, his mom Tracy, dad Doug, his grandma, and his "nanonk," Uncle Travis. (I wondered if nanonk owned Nonk's Car Repair back up Route 329 in Rynela, near the trailer of the lady that advertised "Professional Ironing.")

Trey, in his little jeans and bright red rubber Wellingtons, held his hands on both sides of his head and, with eyes wide as plates, told me about what was "in there." Turkey necks tied to strings and weighed down with washers were the bait of choice of all the crabbers on the dock, and a four-foot gator had decided to come and help himself. He'd just been shooed away and waited on the other side of the canal.

Trey had his own cooler filled with crabs. His parents had a second cooler, so full that when they opened it, crabs spilled out.

Tracy and grandma sat on chairs under striped umbrellas and tried to keep Trey from climbing the dock's fence. Nanonk said, "If'n you fall in, I ain't goin' in after ya. Gonna let the gator git ya."

That night would be America's first 4th of July night since September 11. All through Louisiana we'd seen evidence that people planned to celebrate with spirit. Fireworks stands were busy. But there'd be caution, too. I'd seen a *Times-Picayune* story titled "United We Plan" about security measures to protect celebrations large and small around the country. Americans would be out on Independence Day, but with their guard up.

We stood on the balcony of our Bossier City motel and watched fireworks from Shreveport, just across the Red River. Inside the room, James Taylor and Ray Charles entertained on TV from New York City, and two giant crickets tried, unsuccessfully, to elude me.

## 5

## *INTO THE WEST: Arkansas, Texas, New Mexico*

We started the day with Adam's dream breakfast – steak and eggs at the Waffle House. I'd been denying him this treat across entire states, either because breakfast was included in our motel rate, or because we had enough bagels and peanut butter stashed from previous motels to tide us over.

Route 71 to Arkansas glowed hazy gold in the early sun that rose behind fields of peaches and peas, tomatoes and sunflowers. The earth was red, the grass dewy green. Signs told of yesterday's hot-selling fireworks: "EXPLODING BIN LADEN NOGGINS." Near Gilliam, orange-headed oil wells started to appear in the glistening cornfields. Like birds pecking in the dirt for insects.

We stopped at the Doddridge Post Office, where Rural Carrier Irene Adcock sorted mail before loading it into her Jeep. Homemade flyers on the counter told of missing bird dog Buddy and the Stanley Sisters concert at the yellow, aluminum-sided Victory Tabernacle, which we'd just passed back in Ida, Louisiana. It was at Doddridge, Arkansas that I realized the informational value of the post office. Across the country, there'd be no better place to meet people, ask questions, and learn a little something.

Small, enticing county roads fed off Route 71. If you had an extra lifetime, you could sample them all. Red, red earth. Dead armadillos. The first were a shock. We were to get quite used to them.

We saw Kansas and Iowa plates at the McDonald's in Texarkana. Because they don't get it much, fast food makes

Adam and Dana happy. A little fast food would go a long way - hundreds of miles, I hoped. We were about to cross Texas, so we stopped for hash browns and Egg McMuffins. We drove down Texarkana's Martin Luther King Boulevard. At 9:14, we were in Arkansas. At 9:15, we were in Texas.

Outside Texarkana, the road lost its various names and became just Route 82, a road I came to love. Route 82 would bring us to Wichita Falls, where we'd pick up its identical twin, Route 287, to cross the rest of Texas to Amarillo. We spent two days on these routes, enough time for them to show us Texas' soul. They brought us across the state at 40 miles per hour, a speed that allowed slice of life close-ups of the 50 towns we drove through. Together, these roads that followed the Red River valley were a Main Street that stretched 12 hours. A string that held 500 miles of dusty pearls, from Nash to Amarillo.

We'd left the south's humidity behind and were now enveloped by the west's dry heat, which I hoped would quiet the swelling in my left knee. I'd had surgery in April to repair a running injury and was hoping to start training for a fall marathon while on this trip. July 1, the date my doctor had said I should be able to run again, had come and gone. (I'd attempted a jog that day under the 300-year-old arching trees of Oak Alley, which we'd visited back in Louisiana, but searing pain stopped me cold, and I took that plantation tour in a very depressed state. Dana, who has more empathy in her little being than anyone her size or larger, was equally sad.) The new running target date was July 15. If I couldn't run then, there'd be no marathon. I was banking on Texas' dry heat, like a hopeful pilgrim to Lourdes.

We rode slowly across a Texas of windmills; feed stores; farm equipment; taxidermists; stands selling watermelon, pecans, okra and peas; churches; fences holding cattle and horses; weedy lots filled with rusted machinery, old cars and parts, plane fuselages and grounded houseboats; custom hay baling; arched metal gates guarding ranches like Bar D and Bubba Rosa; bobbing oil wells of

41

all sizes and colors; water towers; cell towers; 19$^{th}$-century brick and sandstone downtowns, frozen in time.

"Welcome to DeKalb – Birthplace of Dan Blocker." The back seats asked, "Who's Dan Blocker?"

"Hoss, on 'Bonanza.'"

"What's 'Bonanza?'"

"The western show with the Cartwrights and the Ponderosa."

Nothing. I hummed the theme song. Nothing. No flicker at the mention of Little Joe or Hop Sing. Dan Blocker's name was written on a huge, faded green sign with graying white letters. The town's gazebo was festooned with vivid, fresh flowers, ardently maintained by the Gardenia Garden Club.

102.5 FM from Texarkana delivered country with attitude. I heard Toby Keith's "Courtesy of the Red, White & Blue" for the first time, with its images of an angry Statue of Liberty shaking her fist at al Qaeda, who'd have "hell to pay."

We pulled into Clarksville's historic old square and parked near the Red River Appraisal office. A Chinese restaurant occupied one of the old pastel storefronts, and the sign at Doughnut Junction, a tiny shop attached to someone's house, let the town know there were more than just donuts in the oven: "We're having twins."

I was worried about New Paint's oil level and had been looking for a full serve station since New Orleans. As I was now a self-pumper who no longer needed full serves, God evidently saw no need to continue putting them in my path. Finally, one appeared, in Blossom, Texas. At Sessum's Conoco, next to the old brick Blossom Hardware building, the mechanic, who'd been working in one of the bays repairing a riding lawn mower, checked the oil and said it was almost full. Fine girl, New Paint. Down not even a quart after 3,200 miles. I told the mechanic I was a little surprised, considering we'd driven from Boston. He peeked into the van to appraise our set-up, noting the strategically located hanging snack bag and the box full of movie videos. He gave an approving smile and said, "Y'all be careful." A customer who'd overheard us and gone back to verify my road trip claim by checking our license plate added, "Yer a long way from home." I hadn't thought much about that until this moment. We'd had places and people and each other to keep us from thinking about the miles between us and home, and they didn't feel far yet.

West of Paris, there were fewer trees and more open land, and around Lannus the earth turned from rich red to deep black. In Savoy, population 850, a blue street sign on Route 82 read, "HIGH WAY." The parking lot of the elementary school, where I stopped to pull some fruit cocktail down from the Thule, smelled heavily of cow. A massive Baptist church was under construction in Sadler. It looked like a religious Wal-Mart Supercenter.

From Whitesboro to Gainesville, Dana left her book on the seat and sat glued to the windows. There were no cows here. Just horses. "Performance Horses," stud farms, Quarter Horses. "I know where to come to buy my horse," marveled Dana, as ranch after amazing horse ranch rolled by. It rivaled Lexington.

We learned to gauge the distance to the next town by looking for its water tower, which almost always bore the name of the school sports team. The Gainesville Leopards, Lindsay Knights, Nocona Indians, Memphis Fightin' Cyclones.

Muenster, a little piece of Germany in Tornado Alley, proclaimed its "100 Years of Gemutlichkeit," friendliness nurtured by long-standing establishments like Fischer's German Sausage, Bayer's Bakery, Rohmer's Restaurant and, hold onto your wiener schnitzel, Flusche Enterprises, purveyors of plumbing and pipe.

In pretty St. Jo, Dairy Queens (the "Texas Stop Sign") started in earnest. Every town of more than a few hundred souls would have one. St. Jo was the place I gave myself permission to sin. By St. Jo, I'd driven nearly three hundred miles since morning, and we weren't done yet. A small vanilla cone is the perfect reward for such an effort, and Dairy Queen is the best place on the planet to eat one. But I had a dilemma. I don't eat between meals. In St. Jo, I amended my rulebook to allow myself a small Dairy Queen cone, for the remainder of the trip, whenever I'd done a whole boatload of driving. I'd applaud my flexibility on this issue from Texas clear through the Dakotas.

Near Electra, Texas became the Texas of my mind. Low, wide, endless. The kids were occupied with *Wayne's World 2*, but I put the windshield visors up to drink in the boundless view. The landscape was a palette of earth tones at once muted and intensely alive – purple, mauve, shades of thick greens, rusts, ochres and tans, deep, rich reds, and grayish blues from the thickening fog. An infinite sky that kissed earth, then bounced up and kept going. Billows of white clouds that started on the ground and soared past heaven. Great cotton geysers. Clouds like giant mittens. Clouds like mountain ranges. Clouds that sat on our heads. Vastness of earth. Vastness of sky.

We stopped for the night in Childress. At the El Sombrero restaurant, where everyone knew everyone, the mayor of Childress moved around to different tables to chat and pick off people's plates. As we waited for our order, he spied Dana and called over, "If you had any food yet, I'd be sittin' over there with you." We sat next to Joe and Pearl. They'd lived in Amarillo, Illinois, Iowa, and Kalispell, Montana, but returned to Childress, Joe's birthplace, to retire. They told us about the giant wild hogs that come out at night. "They send the meat to New York." They recommended we make a (substantial) detour to see some giant outdoor scenes of Jesus' life, but I told them we needed to stay pointed toward Amarillo and Cadillac Ranch, "'Cuz it's the closest these kids'll ever get to Stonehenge." Serious Joe chuckled at that one, but Adam, not a gray area type, later asked why I'd said something that was "a lie."

We had more Texas to cross in the morning. Clarendon invited you to "Stay all night, stay a little longer." Goodnight had a

44

few buildings and a cemetery. Claude's six-cylinder Attebury Grain elevator met the railroad tracks where a Burlington Northern sat waiting to load. Field, road, tracks, field. We'd followed the tracks through much of Texas, and we'd stay with them to New Mexico and beyond. Some ersatz towns had few or no buildings, only track and a sign with the place name. Whistle-stops. Like the Ashtolas, East and West. And East and West Kasota, which flanked Kasota. Why didn't they bundle them up into one Ashtola or Kasota? Why have several when there was barely enough to make one?

Amarillo came, and there was the Big Texan Steak Ranch. Since Claude, we'd seen billboards advertising their "FREE 72-oz. Steak\* *\*if eaten in an hour*," and the filled parking lot at 10 a.m. told of lots of folks inside with loosened belt buckles who'd likely be loosening their wallets by eleven.

Adam and Dana left their names on the spray-painted fenders of Cadillac Ranch. I called Mike as we walked through the fallow field toward the ten cars planted grills-down in the dirt. A bolt from a monster cloud on the horizon heralded bad weather, so we talked and graffitied fast, then drove into New Mexico, where we gained an hour.

Fifty miles from Tucumcari, the orange and adobe-colored land began to thrust itself upward into buttes and mesas, and wilder red rock in the distance promised utter majesty. The patient hand of time had sculpted the earth into art. In Saint Jon, the cemetery's evergreens, all wind-bent in the same direction, were testament that the artist was still at work. Striations of color in the sandstone mountains told of creation working its craft across eons. Younger tan and ochre work rested near summits, ancient cinnamon and richer maroon layers deeper down.

This was a powerfully beautiful world where the ordinary seemed extraordinary. The bewitching headlights of a hundred-car Union Pacific made the train a shimmering mirage as it curved toward us through the desert. We were in a place where a freight train is the most magnificent thing you've ever seen.

In Santa Rosa, where truckers stopped to rest and refuel, we took in the amazing collection of vintage cars and Mother Road memorabilia at the Route 66 Auto Museum and talked with Anna, the owner. Adam and I both burned a roll of film on the gleaming Mustangs and GTOs, DeSotos and Impalas, Bel-Air Nomads and Tom Joad trucks, all with hoods up to show pristine engines.

I asked Dana to take a picture of Adam and me in front of a tomato-red convertible, circa about when I was born. Dana found us in the lens, then put the camera down. "Adam's taller than you!"

At least once a week over the past few months, before excusing himself from the dining room table, Adam would give me a slim-eyed look and say, "I'm taller than you," which, of course, required me to stand up and prove him wrong. I knew the day would come when he'd be right. We always stood eyeball-to-eyeball, not heel-to-heel, because we enjoyed looking into each other's eyes, the one pair saying something like, "I'm not a kid anymore," and the other something like, "Hold on buddy, I'm still your mother." Mike and Dana measured and refereed. I'd been winning by an almost literal hair for a while now.

Hearing Dana's pronouncement, Adam turned to me, grinning. Hugely. Never mind the vintage wheels. He was taller than his mother. If Dana, chief competitor in almost everything in life had said it, then it must be true.

We stood eyeball-to-eyeball. I disregarded the fact that he wore mega-huge rubber-encased Nikes that must have weighed three pounds and lifted him two inches off the floor (the same shoes the Mississippi had wrapped her mud around). I'd be conceding height to him soon enough. Why not now, while we were on a journey that allowed him to be a boy most of the time, but called on him to be a man some of the time. I'd left Boston with a moody teenager. I was standing, 3,700 miles later, next to a beautiful young person I knew I could count on to take his headphones off when the situation asked for it, pitch in, keep cool, and help us through whatever bump in the road we faced. He was the man of the house – or van, or tent, or motel – for 12,000 miles.

"You *are* taller than me. When did that happen?" We all grinned. Dana lined up her sights again and snapped the photo.

With her husband, museum owner Anna also owned Bozo's Auto Repair, just across the road, and still-to-be-restored classics waited over there. Anna said business at the 2-year-old museum was slow. She chalked it up to the combined effects of September 11, Colorado wildfires just north, and construction on Route 66, which was being chewed up outside her door.

She smiled as she told me this, joking about their bad timing in opening this long pursued dream and labor of love. She was a radiant, happy woman, filled with generous spirit and positive energy. She'd had time to talk, as we were the only visitors. But, as we were leaving, dozens of dressed-up people piled in, laughing and hugging - her Santa Rosa High School classmates. It was their 25th reunion, and Anna had invited them all to visit the museum before they went to church together at 6:00. I hope Anna's museum makes it. But if it doesn't, she'll still have all the love that's floating around in Santa Rosa, New Mexico.

We put down literal stakes in the Santa Rosa KOA, across Route 66 from Anna's museum. Our tent was nestled between fragrant cedars. Campground owner Ellen Amato, a Massachusetts transplant, gave me a discount for hailing – and driving - from her home state. I took canned corn and beans and tomatoes down from the Thule, and Dana made chili over the campfire. The kids reconnoitered the parked RVs for other kids, while I strapped on a headlamp and wrote in my journal. We fell asleep to the long trains and whistles of the Burlington Northern Santa Fe and the light drum of blessed desert rain over our heads.

After Santa Rosa, Adam started sitting up front a lot. I had to do some gear reshuffling. The seat-formerly-occupied-by-laptop and the floor in front of it, erstwhile home to a cooler and water jug, now had to remain empty. As did the rear seat, so Adam could roll back there and hibernate if he wanted to, or Dana could move about between the two rear rows, or the kids could sit in the way back, middle seat down as a snack table, and use Playstation or watch a movie. I lost a lot of storage space, but gained a copilot, one who was now taller than me. He didn't talk a lot, and he had his headphones on most of the time, but it was nice to have him there. He even found a way to play video games on the monitor behind him by tilting his seat all the way back, almost flat like a bed (which annoyed Dana because that put his head in her territory), keeping the controls in his lap, and looking at the screen from an odd, painful-looking angle.

"Pueblo of Acoma. You Are Entering Acoma Pueblo Tribal Lands." As we turned onto Tribal Route 38, we left the Albuquerque stretch of I-40 one hour and a thousand years behind. Acoma, "the place that always was," wrapped around us like a desert wind.

"As you walk through my mesa, you will find nothing but total peace," smiled Dale Sanchez, great grandmother, family matriarch, and one of 5,642 remaining full-blooded Acoma. She led us to the top of Sky City, Acoma Pueblo's 400-foot-high sacred heart and spiritual epicenter. Acoma is America's oldest continually inhabited village. Nearly a thousand years ago, native people lived on these 70 acres of high rock. Three and a half centuries ago, Franciscan father Juan Ramirez asked the people to show him the mesa's most sacred spot. Where the main plaza and kiva were, Ramirez built them a Catholic church.

The double rainbow painted on the thick adobe wall of St. Esteban signifies the Acomas' two religions. Dale explained. "Ninety-eight percent of us are Catholic. One hundred percent of us practice our native ways."

"It's all intertwined," she said, and shared examples of how Acoma blend two cultures and religions. Everything is an ingenious, workable marriage. The people celebrate Indian Easter and Christmas a week before the Catholic holidays. Acoma's medicine man is also a priest. The church's floor is hard sand, to signify Mother Nature, and St. Esteban's ceiling timbers are ponderosa pine, felled on Mt. Taylor, north of the mesa. Once felled, any log that touched the ground before it was set in place was abandoned. Niches in the back of the church are for offerings. "Cornmeal, tobacco, water," said Dale. "We leave simple offerings because our lives are simple."

In the cemetery, which is a dusty plateau of white wooden crosses that extends from the church steps out to the sky at the mesa's edge, Acoma are buried coffinless, one atop another. "We don't come into the world in a box and, by golly, we're not gonna leave in one!" exclaimed Dale. She pointed to a hole in the cemetery wall as she talked more of coming and leaving. "We come from a hole called Mother Nature." And, when Acoma die, "the hole is where we go when we leave this world."

Mother Nature stays close to the people, even at home. Acoma never sweep all the dirt from their houses, but leave some just inside the door. "The dirt inside the door is Mother Nature, a magnet to pull your children, friends, family home safely."

Dale opens the church every morning at five, beginning a new day that "always comes back to four." Each day, at four different times, she tosses corn meal to one of the cardinal directions. "This is my daily ritual. My way of life on the mesa." In the morning, she faces east and cries, "Hello, sun!" At dusk,

49

facing west, she bids the sun goodnight. Facing north around 9 p.m., Dale welcomes the moon and the stars. Before bedtime, she faces south: "See you tomorrow, stars and moon."

Acoma society is matriarchal, with land and decision-making falling to a family's youngest daughter, which Dale is. "The tribal council says, 'You are the landowner. You decide,'" said Dale, about times when decisions are called for. Sometimes Dale's decisions affect the lives of her two brothers. Whether they can marry, whether they can have land. It's up to Dale. For her brothers, the pull of Acoma's ancient ways has remained strong. One brother is a doctor, the other a builder who "worked on New York City skyscrapers." Maybe it was the dirt Dale leaves just inside her door, but something had pulled both brothers back to the pueblo, where they now lived.

Dale was no doubt leaving dirt inside her door to pull someone else safely home. Her grandson was serving with Delta Force in Pakistan. "I'm proud of him," she said. When the magnet of Mother Nature does pull him safely back to the pueblo, reunion talk will likely be in Acoma, which Dale, her children and her grandchildren all speak.


We left Acoma's ancient culture and drove into the 1970s. On our way up to Santa Fe on the winding Turquoise Trail, we passed through Madrid, an old coal mining town that's now a peacefully happening hangout for forty- and fifty-something free spirits. Streams of old hippies with money to spend walked the curving highway, which doubles as Main Street, from bed and breakfast to art gallery to café to boutique. It was six o'clock on a Sunday night, and the place was jumpin' and totally tie-dyed. A live rock concert in a parking lot had graying folks in peasant blouses and sandals dancing, swaying, and watching the purple mountains melt into night around them. We could feel the love.

If I win the lottery, I will go to Santa Fe and buy beautiful things. Santa Fe itself is a beautiful thing. The old hands that made my long silver earrings belonged to Margaret of the San Domingo tribe. I would have paid her much more for the slender, beaded pieces than the $12 she asked. Adam, Dana, and I sat in the old plaza, end of the Santa Fe Trail, and took in the mellow, arcaded adobe and all the people who shared this soothing space. Chic ladies in pencil-thin linen pants, ponytailed men, gallery owners and shopkeepers, Indians, cops, cowboys, tourists riding the little sightseeing cars of the Loretto Line.

Beyond the old town, which preserves the city's history and hosts its art, everyday life went on, inside and outside the van. Adam spied a neon yellow '64 El Camino in Aspen Motors' lot. $8,950. He talked like he'd be coming back to buy it. "El Camino. Okay. Nine grand." Dana tossed him an impish "Why do you want an Al Pacino?"

'It's El Camino, Dana."

"It's Al Pacino."

"El Camino."

"Al Pacino."

"El Camino."

Whole chunks of Cerrillos Boulevard passed as I waited to see how long they could possibly go on. I counted 10 more seconds, then shrieked for them to stop. It reminded me of a drive through the Spanish Pyrenees when Dana and Adam were five and eight. I'd tried to interest them in the spectacular snow-capped peaks, but they sat in the back seat calling each other "idiot" and singing "Jingle bells, Batman smells, Robin laid an egg, Batmobile lost a wheel, Joker takes ballet..." Over and over, for 20 winding mountain miles. They pointed dinosaur finger puppets at each other and laughed little devil laughs.

We passed the Indian Hospital and the Santa Fe Indian School, administered by 19 pueblos. During our time in Santa Fe, we'd pass through pueblos and reservations of the Pojoaque, the Tesuque, and the San Ildefonso, who lived near the curving, green Rio Grande. One morning at 8 o'clock, we watched an elderly couple lock their RV and make their way through Tesuque Pueblo's vast, empty Camel Rock casino parking lot. They were dressed to play: striped white golf shirt over an ample belly, cap with farm equipment logo, aqua polyester pants.

When we left the manmade beauty of Santa Fe and its lovely objects, we climbed into the Jemez Mountains and entered soaring red rock. Behind us, the great Sangre de Cristo range lay blue and purple. And all around us on the road to Bandelier, where we would sit alone in high cliff-top caves and consider the ancient people who once lived there, towering, sculpted earth kissed and awed us. Spectacular mesas, high and red. Singular, stunning formations in orange sandstone, crafted by eons of water and wind. God's art gallery, inspiration for the works for sale back on Santa Fe's Canyon Road.

In New Mexico's northwest, things turned dusty and dry. The kids retreated to their music and reading. Dana drew horses, Adam drew Corvettes. They drank sodas, ate Cheez-Its, watched the Kentucky Derby on videotape, played Nintendo. They withdrew from the sparseness outside the windows and coiled into themselves, leaving New Paint and me to stay focused and rolling. I clicked in the tapes I'd made for stretches like this, drumming the steering wheel and singing to stay engaged and alert.

Since Albuquerque, we'd seen signs warning of extreme fire danger. Acoma had banned all fireworks. Santa Fe National Forest was closed. Puye Ruins were off limits. Now, we felt ourselves driving into places still hotter, drier, more dangerous.

There was little or no cell reception along Route 84. By this time, the phone had morphed from a fun novelty I could use to call Mike with "Guess where we ares?" into something useful, a potential safety tool. We'd started into country where towns and people were fewer and farther between, and I missed the reassuring you've-got-service blips whenever they disappeared from the phone screen.

Somewhere beyond Georgia O'Keeffe's old Ghost Ranch, where the kids went into an empty, derelict cabin and were spooked by a "Hello," I stopped at Valdez Chevron. I pumped and went inside to pay.

"Is Valdez the name of this town?"

"No, Tierra Amarilla."

"Ahh, yellow land," I said, looking out at the seared earth.

"Yes,ma'am. Brown, now," said Ben Valdez gently, turning toward the window. It was a tone of acceptance, not defeat. To Ben, it was how life was. To me, it was frightening.

I thought of the two hundred high desert driving miles still ahead this day and asked Ben if he had any coffee. "Not yet. We just ordered our coffee maker. It comes tomorrow, and the supplies Thursday or Friday. So, by this weekend, we will have coffee." I turned his thoughtful, detailed response over in my mind. Was he just gracious, or excited, or did he perhaps think I might wait three days in Tierra Amarilla for coffee? If I'd asked for coffee in some other place, I would have gotten a "no" and maybe a suggestion of where else to try. But here, Ben Valdez and Tierra Amarilla were looking forward to their new coffee machine, and life moved at a patient pace.

"Entering the Homeland of Jicarilla Apache." The homeland was dry as bone, and Dulce, the reservation's main town, held no sweetness. Dulce Lake, behind Dulce Dam, was grass and dust. Adopt-a-Highway stretches remembered tribal members like Assegra Luccero, Sea Willow. The Jicarilla Vietnam vets had adopted another piece of this lonely up-and-down road. From here on, for many days and many hundreds of miles, I kept the headlights on. These roads numbed the brain, and I wanted a fair chance of waking the eyes and reflexes of anyone coming at us on these thin strips of sizzling blacktop.

We'd been climbing on Route 64, and when we plateaued, the natural gas industry took over. On high ground, where I got some Led Zeppelin and Pink Floyd on Big Dog 96.9, KDAG out of Durango, compressors, tanks, wells, pipes, and holding containers sat unmanned in the desert wilderness. Bright white gas worker pickups populated the road, and when we crested one long rise in the highway at noon, we faced a wall of the white trucks, many from Williams Company, parked at a lone, low building marked "Café," twenty-three miles from Bloomfield, in the middle of nowhere. Lunchtime out in the gas fields.

We came to the green San Juan River, which I will always remember and love. The liquid lifeline hosted a valley and basin that would run green and fertile all the way to Farmington. We first met the San Juan at Blanco, the town a wonderful green relief from the yellow desolation, with fertile fields and trees nurtured by the sweet water. The San Juan and its valley formed a long lush strip that my eyes followed to the horizon for hours, and I missed it when it no longer ran beside us.

We'd entered the Navajo Nation. A sign on the Navajo Missions Communication Center asked people to "Pray For Rain." My fire danger radar had been up in earnest for nearly two hundred miles now, and I sensed things were about to heat up for real. I'd checked the maps for alternate routes, should fire close the roads I'd planned to take, the roads that lived within the lines of the Route Narrative. Parts of the Route Narrative might need to be rewritten. KDAG 96.9, "serving the whole Four Corners area," had thanked firefighters for saving homes and urged them to "stay sane and brave." Not a good sign. Out of the frying pan.

Bloomfield and Farmington oozed into each other, like the natural gas industry that holds them together and keeps them alive. With little else around to please the tourist, Bloomfield's Dairy Queen, which we would have jumped at anyway, looked like traveler's heaven behind the heat waves that danced on the blacktop. The vanilla soft-serves made our hours of desert driving feel like a race run once the medal's around your neck. We got larges this time, and Adam lucked out because Dana couldn't finish hers.

Shiprock was the reason we were here in this burning hot Bloomfield-Farmington sprawl. My brother-in-law, Jim, once hiked near Shiprock, a dramatic monolith that rises nearly eight thousand feet and dominates the Navajo Nation visually and spiritually. He spoke of its monumental profile, its remoteness, its deep meaning. I value Jim's opinion on any subject and put Shiprock on my list of things to see if I ever had the chance.

As we drove through the Navajo Nation, we looked on bright blue meat markets selling mutton and lamb to families eating outside on aluminum tables; satellite dishes painted with Indian motifs; a few mud hogans; stores selling two dollar a pack cigarettes; penned sheep; tightly-packed green and gold hay bricks sold from pickups for five dollars apiece; billboards urging teens to practice sexual abstinence; power lines; houses selling "Frye Bread, Sweet Corn, Roast Mutton." And always, there was Shiprock. To the Navajo, Tse Bit` A`i. Rock With Wings.

We drove out of Navajo land on Route 666, the Trail of the Ancients. The road was arrow-straight, and when the colossal monolith was no longer in front of or beside us, it sat in the rearview mitror and remained there, gradually filling less and less of it as we neared Colorado. Dana had been reading for a long time. She looked up and out the window. "Shiprock is still there," she said quietly. Like Acoma, a place that always was. A great ship of stone riding the earth, giving the people a link to the past, a grip on the present, and hope for the future.

# 6

## THE HIGH DRY: Colorado, Utah, Arizona, Nevada

Adam, Dana and I had been gone five thousand miles. Distance, not time, had become our measure. We lost track of the day and date, but never the miles. We felt them all now, some easy and exciting, others long and unchanging, every one showing us something about the country or ourselves. I was driving about 300 miles a day on roads chosen for this journey, and I'd look down other roads, knowing there were 300 different miles to be had by taking any one of them. America's vastness is a wonder. The freedom we have to venture unchallenged into it is a gift. Sharing it with great companions who are also your children is a rare treasure.

The "Welcome to Wonderful, Colorful Colorado" sign was sad irony. The land spread in seared monochrome, like Ben Valdez' Tierra Amarilla. The bushes that still clung to some bit of life were gray.

Signs all over Cortez told how bad things were. The Anasazi Motor Inn said "Pray For Rain," and Century 21 and the Conoco station were thanking God for firefighters.

The parking lot of our Cortez motel gave onto a postcard Rocky Mountain view, so I parked New Paint so she could look, enjoy and be rejuvenated. When I went out the next morning to begin the tasks required before daily takeoff, New Paint sat in the early sun facing the Rockies, and a white truck marked OJIBWE Wildcat Firefighters sat next to her, its driver drinking coffee and working a cellphone. As part of each morning's pre-departure ritual, I'd dump the melted ice from the coolers and send the kids to the motel ice machine for new stocks. There was no way I could throw water away in front of this man, so I hauled the coolers to the room and dumped the old ice in the bathtub, and still felt plenty guilty.

A wildcat firefighter in our motel parking lot meant fire was near. We'd come to Cortez, and Colorado, only for Mesa Verde, and, when we got to the park, parts of it, including Cliff Palace and Balcony House, were closed due to fire threat. Wildfires had now affected us personally.

The only way to see anything was to go with a group on one of the tours they'd patched together and were still allowing to go out. The Park Service wanted everyone in one place, to count heads and ease evacuation should fire start. Both temperature and tempers were high as rangers dealt with frustrated tourists who'd traveled the country and world to get here. We were assigned to a 10:30 departure on a yellow Dolores School District bus to Spruce Tree House on Chapin Mesa. We killed time in the Visitor Center watching a film of Cliff Palace, the closest we'd get to it, and joked with a couple looking through postcards in the gift shop that it would be hard to find one of something we'd actually see.

But Spruce Tree House was magnificent, and the tour had an unusual edge to it because of the tense, frightening circumstances. The minute our school bus filled and the driver pulled away from the Visitor Center, all of us on the bus became a club and started talking. We sat next to a family from San Francisco whose two daughters, baby Hailey and 11-year-old Amanda, both fell in love with Adam. He gave them equal time, bouncing Hailey on his leg during the bus ride, and climbing into an underground Spruce Tree House kiva with Amanda. All the tour kids went down into the cool, dark kiva. I sensed a silent contest taking shape down there after the smallest kids had come up. The older ones stayed in the hole, and I was tempted to ask the other parents if they wanted to wager on whose kid would win the test of wills and be last up the ladder. I'd have put my money on Adam to win and Dana to place.

Sure enough, after the other kids had caved and climbed out, a conversation like this was going on down in the pit:

"You go ahead, Dana."

"No, Adam. You go."

"No, you go up first. I'll follow you."

"Adam, you're just doing this because you want to be last."

"I do not."

"Yes, you do."

"Be quiet, Dana."

"Thanks, Adam."

Dana capitulated, and Adam was last man standing in the kiva.

Our tour group connected quickly because we had similar thoughts. We felt lucky to have nabbed a tour spot. (Becoming rarer by the hour, I imagined tickets being scalped in the parking lot in whispers to families in RVs.) We were optimistic that Spruce Tree House, not the first choice of anyone on our bus, would be "worth it." We were strangely titillated by our flirt with fire. We trusted the rangers, people we'd we never met, to protect us. And, we couldn't wait to see the cliff dwellings, then hightail it out of Mesa Verde.

None of us had missed the hellish landscape on the 15-mile mountain drive from the entrance up to the Visitor Center. Charred, eerie remains of a year 2000 fire covered the mountainsides. Black limbs and trunks. Gray, leafless trees reaching up like skeletal hands. Almost counterintuitive, this already-burned landscape was, in fact, a safe zone. It had no fodder or fuel left, so wouldn't ignite again. It allowed us safe passage into Mesa Verde, and it was safe passage out, should trouble flare.

As we got off the bus at Spruce Tree House, the driver said, "Don't argue with the ranger." I'd already had my share of short-fused rangers that morning and promised to do nothing to provoke ours.

He was candid. This was no ordinary summer at Mesa Verde. Besides sharing dumb questions from tourists ("I had a woman ask me, 'How high is 13,000 feet?'"), the man I'll call Honest Ranger talked of the toll wildfire took on the people who had to work near and around it. To stay on top of the fire situation and keep the park even minimally operational, rangers were working incredible hours. Some had been assigned to the Durango entrance and were commuting two hours roundtrip daily from Cortez.

"At some point, the money just isn't worth it. We feel like it's August already. We're burnt out." He talked about "ranger slump," the condition that usually hits at the end of the summer. Honest's professional advice was to avoid National Parks and ranger programs at the end of August because the rangers are so fed up. "They've just had it. Don't go at the end of the season. Don't." This summer, the Mesa Verde rangers had contracted slump by mid-July.

As we left Mesa Verde, everything felt hotter than when we'd entered – tempers, the land, the air. A breaking point. I was glad to be leaving. As we descended from the 7,000-foot elevation, a spandex-clad figure on a racing bike pedaled up the mountain toward us. His bicycle was weighed down with packs. It was 91 degrees. He was soaked. I respect endurance athletes and, in normal circumstances, would have nodded acknowledgment and good wishes. But I felt a pang seeing this guy. I figured he'd make it up to the Visitor Center, after who knows how many days or weeks on the road, only to be turned away because the tour spots had been sold out. Great quads, bad joss. At least it would be downhill from there.

"Bye, bye, Miss American Pie, drove the Nissan to the San Juan, but the San Juan was high…" Adam and Dana were in the tent, singing their way through a whipping sandstorm. I'd sent them in to hold the tent down with their body weight, while I sat outside watching the red clouds and bent trees and rising river and unpacked gear. We were in Bluff, Utah, alongside our old friend the San Juan, and Mother Nature was kicking her heels up but good.

It was an anxious hour. I was getting ready to tell the kids to sacrifice the tent and hunker down inside New Paint, like Auntie Em and the gang in the storm cellar, when the whirling clouds, pregnant with red sand sucked from the desert then spit back out, passed. We reclaimed our slice of riverside heaven after cleaning a pound of Utah sand from inside the tent. (Dana had used her time in the tent as human ballast to make this optimistic entry in her journal: "Right now we have set camp and are waiting for the wild, gusty, dusty wind of Utah to stop blowing upon us. Today we shall fall asleep in Utah!")

That night, we sat in our folding chairs next to the fire and watched the San Juan. I proposed a game. We'd go around in a circle, and each person would share a memory or thought about the trip. Something meaningful, interesting or fun. A moment, place, person, day, feeling. I figured we'd go around once or twice, chat for five minutes, then do our own things. But the kids surprised and filled me up. We were 5,000 miles and 14 states gone, not yet halfway, and Adam and Dana had a whole Utah night-full of memories to share. I loved everything they loved, not least because they'd loved it. As each person spoke, the others looked into the flames, recalled, and nodded or smiled. Each story drew us closer. Each recollected vignette stoked good feelings - about the trip, about our being together on it. The stars were high in the now clear desert sky when we called it a night, promising to share more around the next campfire.

Our goal next day was Monument Valley, iconic American travel poster landscape. I relish secret places, but if something's cliché, and I haven't seen or done it, I want to, because clichés are millions of valuable opinions.

We were back in the Navajo Nation. We gave our own names- Satellite Dish, Saguaro, Fat Queen, Tiki House, Millipede, Titanic - to the indescribably majestic buttes and mesas of crimson and orange that took our collective breath away. CD players, books, videos were all stashed as we drove Route 163 through Monument Valley. When Mitten Butte appeared, my déjà vu put me in a geography book, and the kids' put them in a "Roadrunner" rerun. Wyle E. Coyote dumped more than a few anvils from the top of that recognizable rock. The Mitten and its companion formations were beyond gorgeous. This sacred, unspoiled landscape was, alone, worth 5,000 miles.

We entered Arizona, still in Navajo country. Arizona route 163 was also Indian 6450, which we took to Kayenta, a small city with trailers and prefab houses, a silver water tower, and white propane tanks sitting like little submarines in everyone's yards. We poked around the Kayenta Trading Post. I didn't find the slide film I was looking for, but I could've bought a huge sack of Premium Quality High Altitude Horse Oats.

The sack reminded me that Kayenta was at 6,000 feet and that it made better business sense in the Navajo Nation to stock oats over slide film. Dana would have joined the tribe and moved here had that been an option, as horses, mainly paints and mustangs, were an integral part of Navajo life. Some roads had "Horse Crossing" signs. Pickup beds loaded with hay were a common sight, sometimes with kids riding atop the bales. (Many families owned small pickups with one seat in the cab, making it hard to strap everyone in as the "Buckle Up Navajo Nation" campaign urged.) Back in Montezuma Creek, Utah, we'd stopped to watch a small group of horses munch on what little was left of the Whitehorse High School front lawn. The horses seemed to be by themselves, with no one tending them. I popped into the post office to ask the postmistress about them. She pursed her lips and shook her head from side to side: "They shouldn't be there, but it's the only place they can find green." Dana notices everything about horses. Everything. An entry in her journal reads: "We also saw five horses grazing on elemntry *(sic)* school grounds. They must have found it exquisite because we saw there *(sic)* manure on the grounds as a compliment."

We read the items on the Kayenta Trading Post's bulletin boards. Like post offices, store notice boards were a good way to pick up information. There'd be a four dollar a head Hip Hop Dance Friday night and a Healing the Nation Motorcycle Rally in August.

We passed the Probation, Parole Services and Peacemaking Division office. Kayenta Bible Church had services and Sunday school in both English and Navajo. We had lunch at Blimpie's at the Teeh'indeeh Shopping Center. *Windtalkers* was playing at the Black Mesa Twin Cinema, and the Burger King next door offered cultural demonstrations. While you ate your fries, you could go inside a hogan or learn about the real Navajo Code Talkers who'd helped America defeat the Japanese in World War II. After September 11, the Code Talkers had issued a statement proclaiming their willingness to serve America again in the fight against terrorism.

All the roadside stands from Kayenta to Kabito flew American flags. The people were a nation within a nation and loyal to both. As we headed out of Navajo land, two ancient women with tough as walnut faces, wearing stunning turquoise necklaces, were hitching up Route 98. Another sold "Kneel Down Bread" from the back of her truck.

The Junction Drive Inn in Kanab, Utah sold frozen lemonade and elk burgers. I'd pulled into the parking lot to read the map, and a white school bus marked "Special Operations Fire Crew" pulled up across the street and disgorged a dirty fire team in green pants, t-shirts, bandanas and boots. They all looked to be in their twenties. They crossed Route 89, lugging white, yellow, and red plastic bags filled to breaking with filthy clothes, and filed into the Kanab Coin Laundry. It was only 10 a.m., so they must have been working all night, somewhere near. After they fed coins into the washing machines, they dispersed through beautiful red rock Kanab to feed themselves. Some bought fast food, some went into the grocery store at the town's main intersection, some sat on curbs next to gas station soda machines. Cleaning their clothes and clearing their heads before they had to jump back in.

From Kanab, where I bought film from an unsmiling shopkeeper whose unsmiling teenage children all sat in the back of the dark store and stared at us while the transaction was completed, it was a short drive to the crimson glory of Zion. Monstrously hot. Hiking would have been masochism or worse, so we took in the majesty from New Paint's air-conditioned insides. Signs all over Zion warned "NO CAMPFIRES," and major parts of the park were closed to personal vehicles because of fire danger. The heat hung so heavy, it was as if it had become matter. Dana described its penetrating intensity: "It hurts your eyes." You could feel the land ready to ignite.

When we got to La Verkin, fire brewed on a mountainside, and two small planes circled above. I headed for the next post office. In Toquerville, with its neat, solid Mormon church, a fixture in every town since Kanab, I chatted with a guy who'd come in to check his post office box. He told me the wildfire was brand new. "It started about an hour ago. First one in this area." Planes had already dropped retardant. Postal clerk Glade Peterson came back from his break. He opened the counter window and joined the conversation. "Yesterday's lightning must've started it. Dry lightning storm." The fire had been smoldering since yesterday and had just broken through. We got on I-15 and drove toward Cedar City, watching the fire and the small planes that dumped loads of red slurry. The fire sat on our left, between Browse and Pintura, and was growing rapidly.

As we drove, in the same instant, Adam, Dana and I saw something. In the hills to our right, above a beautiful red-sided horse ranch with a green field under irrigation, we saw a fire being born. A whisper of flame and smoke, barely noticeable. I called 911 on the cellphone. "Someone's on the way," said the dispatcher, and, less than a minute later, we watched a state trooper and a pickup outfitted with hoses and a water tank make their way, lights flashing, right up the grass and into the field to the new blaze.

We crossed the southern Nevada desert on a morning when forecasters up in Vegas promised 110 degrees. I knew we were in for a challenge when we hit Modena, Utah. On the map, it looked like a sizeable border town, and I'd planned to fill up there and take a mental deep breath before we jumped into Nevada.

In real life, Modena sat in an elbow-shaped depression off Route 56. We looked down on its tiny entirety from the highway, and I saw nothing inviting. The Nevada crossing was the only point in the trip I'd had any concern about, as the map showed few towns and great, hot distance between them. Looking down on Modena, it hit me that maps are collections of comparisons. Whether something's written big or small on a map depends on what's around it that cartographers compare it to. Modena was near nothing, so they wrote it big. That doesn't mean it has a gas station. If it did, I didn't see it.

We came to the Nevada line and entered eight hours of utter brown desolation. Leaving Utah felt like stepping off into a giant superheated void. This was the trip's longest day.

Through all of Nevada, we'd climb about 1,500 feet to the crests of 6,000-foot summits, plateau at that elevation for a while, then drop 1,500 feet to do it all over again. We crested Panaca Summit at 6,719 feet, then coasted about 10 miles downhill into the town of Panaca. We needed gas. We had half a tank and all of Nevada in front of us. Like Modena, Panaca was big on the map. And, it was the last place writ large for a long, long stretch. If Panaca didn't have gas, we were in trouble.

The town was a shock. Route 319 cut through downtown, where we saw not a soul. There was Panaca Market, a Mormon church, and the Spud Shop, which sold something called spudnuts. No gas station. Was this a joke? Were we in a bad dream? People could buy spudnuts in Panaca, Nevada, writ big on the map, but no gas? My hands clammed up on the steering wheel as I looked clear to the end of Panaca where Route 319 dead-ended at Route 93. I knew we couldn't leave this town without buying gas, because the map showed a whole lot of hundred-degree nothing beyond it. I made plans. I'd call AAA on the cell phone and have them deliver. I'd flag down passing cars and pay them to siphon gas into New Paint's tank. I'd find a local rancher and buy up his supply of tractor gas.

Just as I had us putting down temporary roots in Panaca, ("Hi, Mike, it's us. Just wanted to let you know we'll be a few days late meeting you in Fort Bragg because we're living in Panaca, Nevada until we find gas.") an old service station appeared. It was a full-serve. I laughed out loud, because New Paint needed an oil check, too. Hot dang. Good joss, this!

Two guys were working under the hood of a white pickup. We sat at the pumps for a few minutes, waiting to be full-served. We were three feet from these guys. Neither looked up. There was an old man inside the station. He didn't come out. I got out of the van and waited. Nothing. I popped the hood and stood there. Not so much as a "be with you in a minute." Adam got out of the van and stood next to me. We were invisible. "I guess we'll have to figure out how to check the oil," I said so they could hear. Nothing. None of the three grown men at this blistering outpost paid any attention to a woman traveling across the desert with two children. Yes, this was a joke, and we *were* in a bad dream.

I filled the tank and went inside to pay. A trio of slovenly, overweight people was stocking up on 9:30 a.m. chips and soda. The leathery old man behind the counter took my money without looking up. He said nothing. I read all the signs and newspaper clippings he'd tacked up. I figured he wanted me out of there, so I took my time. "Dear IRS, Please Cancel My Subscription." "If you're grouchy or ornery there'll be an extra $10 charge for puttin' up with you." "It's easy to call branding inhumane when you're sipping wine in Las Vegas." And the handwritten chart showing mileage between Panaca and other populated places. Beyond nearby Pinoche and Caliente, every other place was triple digits away. I went outside feeling bad. We'd just started Nevada, and it hadn't shown us anything good.

When I got to the van, one of the guys who'd been working on the pickup had just finished checking the oil and coolant and was teaching Adam how to do it. He told me everything was full, that everything "looked good." That was all. No other conversation, no questions, no lingering.

But that's all that was needed to redeem Nevada.

## 7

## *GOLD AND GOLDEN: California*

"Where're you comin' from?" asked the officer at the California Agricultural Inspection Station.

"Today, Cedar City, Utah."

"Where'd you start?"

"Boston."

"Got any fresh fruits or vegetables?"

"Just apples from motel breakfasts - and canned stuff up top."

"Go on through, and drive safely."

This was Benton, population 164. We climbed up out of it, looking down on a hot spring and the Benton Paiute Reservation, and started through a strange high altitude landscape that married desert and mountains. The snow-topped Sierras sat ahead of us as we made our way across a mountain plateau seasoned here with desert scrub, there with pine needles and cones. It was a landscape in molt, changing from parched desert to alpine peaks. No longer one, not yet the other. Wild, lonely Route 120 took us along for the metamorphosis.

When the transition to mountains was complete, the narrow road dropped us in the Sierra town of Lee Vining, gateway to Yosemite and tufa-pillared Mono Lake. We were beat. The long days of desert, rock, heat, fires and vast dryness had sapped us. We craved coolness. Freshness. Trees. We needed to stretch and eat and be entertained in spaces larger than New Paint's three rows of seats. We needed to spread out and have more than two feet between us. We needed community. We needed to just hang for a while. Lee Vining fit the bill. Laid back, full of friendly locals. And serious fishermen, who'd already scored most of the motel rooms.

I sent my third installment to the paper from an Internet connection in a building that did triple duty as bookstore, tourist office and headquarters of the Mono Lake Committee. They had sample "Save Mono Lake" letters to Governor Gray Davis printed in soy-based inks on 100% recycled paper. Caltrans, the state transportation department, planned to widen Route 395, which ran through Lee Vining and above Mono Lake. Locals were concerned about the effects on the fragile salt lake's alkaline ecosystem. Caltrans was a demon. Besides fishing, it was the main topic of conversation, whether at breakfast at Niceley's or dinner at Bodie Mike's, named for Bodie, the ghost town at the end of an unpaved mountain road northeast of town. If people weren't talking about salmon egg bait or catching their limit in trout, they were talking about Caltrans and the Draft Environmental Impact Report.

Kelly Cashman had one room left at the El Mono Motel, attached to her Latte Da Café. She checked us in at the café cash register while ringing orders of oversized muffins and organic coffee and tea. She'd check us out the same way, multitasking between departing motel guests and her regular early morning breakfast crowd, who were talking passionately about Caltrans.

I loved when I could park New Paint just outside the motel room door. The green machine was one of us, and I liked to see her there near the window. Parked tail in, I could lift the tailgate and make her and her contents an extension of the room, so we could leave almost everything packed, and go out when we needed something.

The lifted tailgate sparked conversation as people stopped to look at the stacking boxes, then our license plate, the Thule, the coolers, the drying laundry, us. I'd watch them conclude that we were on the road for a while. They'd start talk with, "How long you been gone?" or "Where you headed next?" Soon, they were sharing stories.

Americans wanted to see America. It was an almost universal feeling. Waitresses in breakfast joints, store cashiers, front desk clerks, motel guests, people we met at restaurants and gas stations and post offices and boat docks – nearly everyone had the same reaction when they learned what we were doing. Some told of cross-country trips dreamed of but not yet taken. Others talked of friends or relatives who'd gone cross-country. Some had done it themselves.

Like Don, the erudite maintenance man at our motel back in Morgan City, Louisiana. We'd met Don, a retired AT&T man, in the parking lot, where we were dodging giant armored bugs the size of wallets. When one flew like a bird, right next to my head, I screamed. "Tree locusts," explained Don. "Used to make the whole community roar, but now humans have come in and displaced them." We stood for a while by the swimming pool fence and swapped road stories. Like so many people, Don thought Dana and Adam inestimably lucky to be having this experience. Nostalgia brought Don back 50 years to when he crossed America as a teen in 1953. He'd driven a Nash Ambassador with no air conditioning and had dealt with the 120-degree California desert by crossing it at night. "Haven't forgotten the trip to this day," he said quietly, looking at the ground, then at the kids, remembering.

I'd heard some great road trip stories before we left home. My favorite was from Bruce, the ex-cop who used to cook at Main Street Café at the end of our street. Bruce was a breakfast bartender. He served pancakes and conversation.

He told me about the cross-country trip his parents had taken when they were in their 70s. His dad was a big guy, with weight issues. When Bruce and his sister were kids, they'd hide snacks in their bedrooms to keep dad from eating them before they got any. Dad would walk to the store to "get a paper," and down a bag of chips on the way home. When he was on Weight Watchers, and "those points just weren't enough to satisfy him," he'd hide emergency peanut butter in the bathroom.

Bruce's parents, "in a conversion van, with beds," called regularly from the road. His mother would always dial and talk before she handed the phone to dad.

"So, how's Memphis, mom? Seen Elvis?" Mom would tell of the sights, then say, "Here, let me put your father on."

"So, how's Memphis, dad?"

"Well, I just had a hush puppy. It was delicious!"

In St. Louis, mom exclaimed, "And there's the Gateway Arch, right over there! Here, let me put your father on."

"I just had the best barbecue sauce I've ever tasted! They make barbecue sauce really different down here!"

Mom called from Galena, Texas. "How's Texas, mom?" Mom described the landscape and attractions and said, "Here, let me put your father on."

"How's Texas, dad?"

"Well, I just had the greatest steak! They make beef different here. They raise the steers different!"


Our stay in Lee Vining had recharged us. We headed toward Tahoe on 395, passing through crisp Sierra towns cradled by snowy peaks. The icy beauty made us forget wildfires and blast furnace weather. We drove, thinking Lee Vining thoughts: listening to fish tales about big ones pulled from Tioga Creek; sprawling on the motel bed in front of the TV to watch the Calgary Stampede; walking the town's tree-covered neighborhoods past the small wooden houses; playing video games and pool in the backroom of Bodie Mike's. While Adam and Dana played, I'd sipped wine and talked with Brynne, the bartender. She'd given the kids run of the backroom as long as they didn't come near the bar. I brought their Cokes to them at the pool table. Brynne, studying to be a physical therapist, would inherit Bodie Mike's someday. She was marrying the owner's son: "Took eight years to get a ring." After Lee Vining, we were renewed. Even New Paint took to the road with sparked vigor.

But the heat didn't let go for long. We'd feel it again before we hit Tahoe. Antelope Valley's Walker River ran beside us for a while. Clear, green, and bouncing fast and white over tan rocks. It led to the town of Walker, its mountainsides burned. Three virgin wildfires were building strength in the hills above the road. At Coleville, bad went to worse, and the earth was on fire again.

Coleville High School had been turned into a firefighting command center. Two fires raged. And they got bigger, before our eyes, gaining on us most of the way to Tahoe.

A card table marked "Check In " sat at the high school's front door. Inside the fenced-in schoolyard, workers catching a break ate from Stewart's Firefighter Food Catering trailer. A water tanker driver slept in his cab, boots sticking out the truck's window.

It was a big operation. Signs at the command center thanked "Marines, Pilots, Firefighters, Law Enforcement." Planes circled the fires, and a massive Chinook dropped loads of retardant from a huge, hanging red bucket. It was eerie to be in the thick of this. We were glued to the windows, watching the fires spread and water tankers race south toward us on 395 out of Reno, Nevada. People had started to pull off the road to sit it out and watch. Everyone's headlights were on. The smoke cloud chased then caught up with us. It blocked out the sun and took on the look of an atomic blast- orange, yellow, sick gray and brown. I stopped to take pictures. We'd never see the likes of this again, so close. Dana shouted, "My seat is red!" The dashboard was orange, the road and cows outside the van a frightening shade of fiery crimson.

At Topaz, California, population 100, we drove above Topaz Lake, elevation 5,050 feet. The lake below us was peppered with weekend boaters and jetskiers who flitted about in noon darkness, the water and air turned gray by the gargantuan smoke clouds that would soon send everyone indoors. People were eking out a last bit of Sunday fun before the fire put an end to it. It was surreal. People buzzing about on fast boats, and water-skiing, while a hideous mountain of flame, ash and smoke bore down and ate more of the land just beyond the lake. I looked at the water the people played in and thought if it could only be lifted up and delivered to the hills, it might be enough to stop the fiery advance.

At the state line, cars traveling south from Nevada waited at the California Agricultural Inspection Station, everyone looking up at what they were driving into. The air was heavy with the smell of burning pine. Tiny pieces of ash floated around New Paint and settled wherever they could take hold. The day turned brown.

We rode down into Nevada's Carson Valley, through Gardinerville and old, brick Minden. Sierras embraced us. The fire followed us.

"Tahoe Horse Shows in the Sun," said the sign. From the road, I'd seen a few riders fly over jumps. I pulled into the show site. "Any chance this young horse lover from Massachusetts might watch for a few minutes?" I asked the old man sitting under an umbrella by the dusty parking lot. "Go on through," he smiled.

This was serious stuff. Professional riders, wealthy owners, incredible equines. The scene was moneyed, electric, regal, privileged. And surreal.

As these impeccably-postured people and equines flew, seemingly without effort, around the arena and over the jumps, as rapt owners and spectators watched every turn and hoofbeat, two wildfires raged not more than a score of miles away. The fire we'd driven under was eating the sky to the right of the small grandstand, and a second fire, wholly in Nevada, was gaining momentum and height to the left. No one looked at, spoke of or paid any attention to the wildfire-filled sky. They rode and watched their horses. Over our heads, firefighting tanker planes came and went, landing at an airstrip next to the show site, reloading with slurry and water, and taking off again. And again, and again, and again, while people rode five-figure horses and tried to win blue ribbons.

It wasn't until we climbed the Kingsbury Grade that we lost sight of the fires. The Kingsbury Grade is an engineering marvel that starts in Carson Valley and climbs the wall of Sierras that hold Lake Tahoe. When we crested 7,334-foot Daggett Summit, we were on the lip of the wall, and Carson Valley and the fires behind it disappeared as we descended toward the cobalt lake.

When we reached Tahoe's shore, I had no patience for Stateline, a blight of development. I couldn't leave fast enough. And, because of the snarl of vehicles and pedestrians, we couldn't leave at all. The traffic and tourist-choked road and intersections kept us prisoners of Stateline for what felt like a hellish eternity. By the time we broke free, I was ready to pull out my hair. Adam and Dana let me be while I popped my cork. They thought Stateline was cool, and, had they been running this expedition, we would have checked into the next motel on the strip. They hadn't seen half this much action since New Orleans. My last gasket was ready to go when we eased into our tent site at Camp Richardson. A spectacular stand of pines towered over us while we pitched camp, and I calmed down.

Our Tahoe time was spent outdoors. We swam in the cold lake, rode horses, watched purple sunsets, cooked chicken, corn and onions over the fire. On July 15, I ran. I took the knee for a test ride under the pines for about two and a half cautious miles. The knee felt busy, but it didn't hurt, and I was happy.

Dana was waiting at the tent when I got back. "How was your run?" she asked in her sweet, expectant voice, so utterly filled with love. This girl had woken with the sun to wait and see how her mom made out. "It was okay. I think I'll be able to train for the marathon. I'll have to take it slow, but I think the knee is healed." Dana, at 6:30 a.m., in the oversized t-shirt she wore as jammies, hugged me under the pines and said, "That's good." I knew she'd been worried, and hopeful. And I knew my success this morning would bring her happiness all through the day.

Dana's quiet selflessness was as important a piece of equipment on this trip as anything we'd packed. Her steady, gentle way smoothed our human dynamics. We knew each other so well, that we sometimes forgot to consider or be patient with one another. Sometimes we put I before we, behavior not sustainable on a long trip in close quarters. Sometimes we were too big for the van we rode in or the motel room we shared. Dana would, more times than not, become the beach on which our emotional waves broke and dissipated, being calmly absorbed or redirected, allowing the flow of our journey to continue.

Late in the night, Tahoe's coyotes screamed. They gathered in wetlands off Pope Beach Road and howled maniacally. A chilling, frenzied sound that made you pray dawn would come fast.

On our last evening, Adam raced to the tent with Jared and Carlos, two Sacramento boys he'd met, to tell me a 4-year-old boy was lost, and everyone was going out to search.

People appeared between the trees, calling, "Andy! Andy!" The police were out, and campers were searching on foot and bike. Andy was autistic, which made the tense situation extremely grave. A young Filipino man, Andy's uncle, walked through our site, searching for the boy and enlisting help. He told me Andy could hear rescuers' voices, but wouldn't be able to respond. He might be 10 feet from a savior, but wouldn't be able to let that savior know he was there.

I started searching the woods off Pope Beach Road and met the camp host, a guy who gets a trailer site with hookups for the summer in exchange for minimal duties. He was coming up out of the swampy wetlands. He lived here and knew the territory. "I hope he didn't wander off in there," he said. "There's a pack of coyotes in there who tear geese apart at night and howl like the *Silence of the Lambs.*"

"They found him! They found him!" Two hours after he disappeared, 4-year-old Andy was reunited with the people who loved him. All of Camp Richardson gave thanks.

We left Tahoe and followed the beautiful Truckee River to I-80 and the mountains that did in the Donner Party. The scenery was superb, and we watched trains cut across high cliffsides on tracks covered by roofs to keep winter's snow buildup at bay. Service area signs offered food, fuel and "chain services," suggesting the Donner Party, if not properly outfitted for winter, might have trouble getting through today, even in a truck.

It was on I-80 that I felt the first pull of the sea. We were days away from the Pacific, but had started the descent out of the Sierras. On a long, beautiful downhill off Donner Summit, signs warned truckers, "Save Your Brakes. Let 'Er Drift. Let 'Em Cool." I took the advice, sat back, and coasted. "We're on our way to the ocean, guys."

"And daddy," whispered Dana, looking off into the distance, as if imagining what he would look like running toward us in Fort Bragg to gather us up in his arms.

We got off the interstate and took Route 20, a single lane highway that would carry us most of the way across California. The highway changed with the elevation, taking us out of high wilderness down to where the land lost its mountains. It was first a National Forest Scenic Byway, with huge pines hugging the road and vast mountain vistas. Then, it was an artery feeding the huge agribusinesses of the Sacramento Valley. It ended as a winding meander past the string of laid-back lake towns that sit east of the Russian River, the Redwood Empire, and the Mendocino coast.

Latino pickers, wrapped against the sweltering sun in hats, face scarves, pants, long sleeves, and gloves, tended hot fields. Endless alleys of Diamond walnuts, almonds and pecans; strawberries and blackberries; peaches, plums, apricots and nectarines; tomatoes, peppers, cukes and avocados; lemons, melons, grapes and cherries; pears, sweet corn and sunflowers. The Sacramento Valley was wickedly dry, yet still bountiful.

Earlier, we'd detoured into the Gold Rush. The towns of Nevada City and Grass Valley overflowed with magnificent sherbet-hued Victorians, built by Cornish miners to resemble cottages back home. The hilly towns were nonstop eye candy, and I could have walked their streets for days.

At Empire Mine, 350 miles of underground passages and once California's richest hard rock gold mine, we stood at the top of the slanted shaft and peered down a minute stretch of Empire's 11,000 feet of total incline depth. Cold air from the bowels of the earth washed over us. Workmen from Gray Electric were in the shaft, building a simulated ride that the foreman explained "will make visitors feel like they're hurtling down in the carts that brought the miners down." It was to open at the end of the summer.

"Oh, man!" moaned Adam, lamenting missing this high-speed jolt down into a cold, dark hole in the earth. "We should've come here in August!"

I would have liked to go down into Empire, too, not for the hurtling, but to listen to a mine's ghosts. To hear in the empty tunnels and caves and niches the voices and labored breathing of men, the clink of axes picking slowly and ceaselessly at unforgiving walls of rock, the rattle of pony carts, the drip of water from stone. The grim underearth sounds of men wresting something people deem precious from brutal, sunless holes. Descending into a black mine only lets you begin to grasp the bleakness of a miner's day and lifetime.

We'd gone down into an old coal mine back in Beckley, West Virginia, where I'd reminded Adam and Dana of their great-great-grandfather, John Delbridge Pille, a Cornish tin miner who'd come to America to mine coal outside Pittsburgh, not all that far as the crow flew from Beckley. Jim, who'd been a miner for 38 years, was our Beckley guide. His grandfather, father, sons, and grandsons had also spent years of their lives underground, working the soft coal of the Sewell seam. We'd traveled in converted coal cars on tracks, down and through the dank pitch of Beckley's drift mine, nearly horizontal and far closer to the surface than the steep maw of the Empire, at whose entrance, 4,600 miles from Beckley, we now stood.

Jim had pointed out hand-hewn alcoves, some no more than three feet high, telling us to imagine stooping or lying on our backs, swinging a pick for eight hours to loosen the coal overhead. He'd talked of killers unleashed as men cut coal. Methane, released from seams that had held it for ages, exploded. Seeping poison gas displaced fresh air and killed quickly, creating deadly pockets called black damp. Canaries would succumb before humans, so if a miner's bird died, the man knew he had but a few minutes to escape the area of fouled air.

Now, as I stood before Empire's steep lip, I wondered if John Delbridge Pille, tin and coal miner, had known any of the Empire gold men. Empire's success had been built in no small part on the skill and experience of Cornish tin and copper miners who'd left England at the news of California gold. Pille had left England for Pittsburgh about 1840, only a decade before Empire's first Cornwall miners arrived. Maybe some of the men who'd worked a mile or more down in the cold hole we now stood at had once worked beside my great-grandfather, pulling tin from one of the mines whose stone wheelhouse ruins dot the Cornish landscape like crumbled industrial cathedrals.


The ocean called. It wouldn't lap us today, but likely tomorrow. There were only two dates on this trip when we had to be somewhere, both related to Mike's coming and going. We had to meet him in Fort Bragg after his plane in, and deliver him to Billings before his plane out. We were on track to beat Mike into Fort Bragg by a wide margin, the result of a continent's worth of early "up-and-at-'ems." To me, 9 a.m. meant fifty to a hundred miles already tucked under New Paint's wheels. Because we'd been up and out early nearly every morning since Pennsylvania, we had some extra time built up, and the exit for Rough and Ready was too intriguing to pass by.

We climbed past roads like Cattle Drive, Grubstake Trail and Ironclad Road to reach "The Great Republic of Rough and Ready," flags of the republic flying next to Old Glory. Rough and Ready, California seceded from the Union in 1850, angry over a mining tax on gold claims. Three months after secession, on the 4th of July, it rejoined the nation in a fit of patriotic fervor (or dawning of economic reality?).

We sent postcards from the former Republic, population 1508, elevation 1805 feet (had a lottery been at hand…), and I took pictures of the old W.H. Fippin Blacksmith Shop (the date, again, 1850 – oh, where was the lottery?). A crusty, ancient man pulled out of the post office parking lot across the street and stuck his head from the window of his sputtering, orange Dodge Tradesman van. He bobbed his head up and down and called, "Old blacksmith. I quit workin' there 21 years ago today." Then he waved and disappeared. Was it possible that the Fippin blacksmith shop was still operational in 1981, and this guy had worked old William Fippin's shop? Or, had we just seen a flippin' ghost who was telling me he *was* the old blacksmith? "That's really scary," said Dana, as "The Flippin' Ghost of Rough and Ready" entered our stock of trip lore and legend.

Rough and Ready's Wayside Chapel was for sale by Grass Roots Realty. A banner across the old brick Cramer Building pronounced it the "Rough and Ready Opry House, Home of the Fruit Jar Pickers." Mason Kerr-Atlas and the Ball Brothers entertain On The Porch, Sundays, from ten to noon. Everything about the town later confirmed, except the flippin' ghost, I left the former republic of Rough and Ready thinking the whole hamlet was pulling everyone's collective leg. It must be fun, most of the time, to live in an oddball place. Sustained offbeatness requires humor and participation. Maybe the flippin' ghost was playing his role in the Rough and Ready pageant. His job might have been to whisper "Old blacksmith," then disappear, whenever tourists stopped to look at W.H. Fippin's shop.

Dana had run out of reading material. A voracious reader, she'd packed enough, 99 percent horse-related, to last 6,000 miles. By Ukiah, she needed more, and The Tack Shop appeared. Dana bought herself *Happy Horsemanship* and picked up loads of free magazines with pictures of horses and ranches for sale. She sat in the middle seat and dreamed as we rolled toward the ocean.

"Mom, is $100,00 expensive for a horse ranch?"

"It depends."

"What *is* expensive for a horse ranch?"

"It depends." We had a quick economics lesson and reviewed the principle of location, location, location.

Outside Elk, population 250, elevation 140 feet, we reached the Pacific. We'd crossed America.

Adam, Dana and I stood together for a long while. We didn't say much, just stared out across the water and gathered our thoughts. The shimmering ocean crashed onto the beaches below us and into the headlands we stood on. I parked New Paint so she could look out and enjoy the fruits of a continent's worth of labor. I left "we're at the Pacific" messages for Mike and my mother, who I'd last called from Basalt, Nevada, and probably shouldn't have. Moms worry when their children, even 44-year-old ones, are out in the desert, especially if they've got the grandkids with them. The Pacific Ocean message would ease her mind and let her turn her copy of the Route Narrative, which she'd hung on her refrigerator, to a fresh, new page.

The Pacific was a herald, a touchstone, a validator. We soaked in her meaning. We'd reached a geographic milestone. We'd soon turn east, toward home, and head back across America. We'd see Mike in a few days. We'd traveled together in a small space across a whole continent and were still enjoying our adventure, and one another. The country, coast to coast, was vital, united, proud. We stood in the sun, high over the ocean, and took in what she told us.


"Sleep! We get to sleep!" Adam flung himself on the bed at the Tradewinds motel in Fort Bragg, our home until Mike would drive up from the San Francisco airport to meet us. "Yeah, until 8:30." I had to set a limit, or Adam would go teenager, and we'd be breakfasting at lunchtime.

The fridge and microwave in our room presented exciting dining possibilities that we hadn't realized how much we'd missed over the 6,000 miles of eating shaped by coolers and campfires, Sterno and tin cans, and the need to keep moving. Our little Tradewinds home allowed three days of dining in. Frozen things. Leftovers. A vacation from cans. Food that was really hot– or really cold. "Let's go to Safeway" became our Fort Bragg mantra. The North Coast's beaches and seal coves, tide pools and pygmy forest, headlands and lighthouses, towns and trails were magnificent, and we explored them all, but Safeway pulled us in several times a day.

By our first evening, we'd all identified our most urgent unrequited cravings, and we cruised our favorite aisles, filling the shopping cart with beautiful edibles. Chicken pot pies, frozen pizza and TV dinners; bananas and strawberries; cool cups of yogurt; fresh salad fixings; frozen burritos; deli meat, cheese, smoked salmon and shrimp cocktail; chocolate pudding, rice pudding, cottage cheese; fat olives and hummus; cereal and milk.

We kicked back. Slept until 8:30, ate in front of the TV, stayed up past 10.

Fort Bragg grew on us. A big, rough-edged town bounded by smaller, classier neighbors like Mendocino, Fort Bragg works hard for a living, milling lumber and pulling fish from the sea. The Georgia-Pacific plant occupies the lion's share of the downtown coast, and we could pick out Fort Bragg from a dozen miles away by the great, gray smoke plumes that blow from the plant's chimneys night and day and waft out over the ocean.

Mike called to report he'd dropped Dana's fish and bonsai at my parents' house for safekeeping and was itching to get on the plane west. I'd booked him a ticket into San Francisco and out of Billings, Montana, and a Hertz car to get him up to meet us. The nearest Hertz drop-off site was a day north of Fort Bragg, at the Eureka-Arcata airport, so we'd be en caravan along the Avenue of the Giants and the rest of redwood country, boys in the rental, girls in New Paint.

The days waiting for Mike were slow-paced and mellow. We caught up on sleep and hot showers, laundry and email, and the kids got in three nights of instant messaging with their friends, logging on about 4 p.m., which was prime early evening chat time back home. Main Street Cafe had tacked my articles on the bulletin board, and Adam and Dana's friends had read them and seen the kids' pictures in the paper, so they were minor celebrities.

As they typed away, answering friends' questions about where they were and what they were seeing, I sensed their appreciation for the trip deepen.

When we weren't lounging in the room, or picnicking on a North Coast beach, or cruising Safeway, we were hanging around town. In Noyo Harbor, hub of Fort Bragg's fishing industry, the sportfishing side of things was strangely quiet. We looked in on the commercial fishermen and the fish processing and packing operations that lined the weathered wharves, but no one was out at the piers that advertised deep-sea fishing adventures (and school field trips and burials at sea).

"Is business a little slow?" I asked the young woman who sat alone in one enterprise's booking office, the sea-going fishing boats all tied up tight in the channel out back.

"Yeah. Fort Bragg shut down all the salmon sportfishing for two weeks. But we can still do rock cod and albacore!"

How strange, I thought, that we three looked like a real catch on this slow day. We were a lady with two kids. Dana wore a horse t-shirt, we had open-toed sandals on our feet, no hats to keep the sun off, no jackets, and I had my old Nikon and assorted lenses slung around my neck and shoulders. I didn't think we looked ready for or interested in five hours of deep ocean fishing.

"Why no salmon fishing?"

"Oh, there were reports that sportfishermen were using barbed hooks."

An illegal and not very sporting way to reel in the area's coho, chinook and steelhead.

"But, we'll be totally open on Saturday!"

"And how does business look after Saturday?"

"Oh, we're all booked up!" Good. They didn't need me to book a rock cod trip.

On a headland near the College of the Redwoods coastal campus, a dude in a red t-shirt, baseball hat and jeans stood on a cliff near the guardrail, just in front of where I'd parked New Paint. He played the guitar and sang to the ocean. He wailed into the waves and let his chords rip over the sea grass. Behind him, and right next to us, a tan, toned couple in their fifties sat in a flashy silver Audi. The wife watched the guitar player and the blue Pacific. The husband manhandled his building contractor via cellphone. Seems construction of the home theater was behind schedule, and the guy in the Audi was busting a vein. His wife never moved her eyes from the guitar player in the red t-shirt.

You can see the ocean from everywhere in Mendocino. At the farmer's market, where Adam bought honey sticks and people played fiddles and women wore braids and therapists set up massage chairs, I said hello to the guy from Stella Cadente Olive Oil Company. "I feel like I know you. You adopted-a-highway back in Boonville." I told him about our trip and the various ways I tried to learn something about places we passed through. Post offices, radio stations, grocery store bulletin boards, Adopt-a-Highway sponsors. All gave hints about the people who lived in a place, what they did, what the place was about. It was telling that Boonville, population 750, elevation 400 feet above the not-too-distant sea, had its stretch of Route 128 sponsored by a small company that nurtured olive trees and bottled their fruit's oil. The Stella Cadente Adopt-a-Highway sign helped me understand Boonville, "Home of the Panthers," and its Anderson Valley neighbors. This place was about the land and what it could be made to yield. Anderson Valley Brewing Company's field of golden premium barley, Gowan's bounteous produce for sale in Philo, the line-up of vineyards on tiny Route 128- they all made better big picture sense because an olive oil producer had adopted a stretch of local highway.

Up the street from the Mendocino farmer's market, a yard sale billowed beyond the driveway and onto the neat flower-bordered lawn. The only yard sale I've ever gone to that had an ocean view. Other browsers bought the used clothes and curtains and books, but I found California things. An abalone demitasse cup and a ceramic bowl shaped and painted to look like an open artichoke.

Mike came.  He found us at Fort Bragg's Pudding Creek Beach under the high, old wooden trestle bridge, and he and the kids ran through the sand and splashed in the tide pools and laughed and rolled down the tan sand hills. We spent one more night in Fort Bragg, then drove up the coast and into the redwoods, boys in the little white rental following girls in New Paint.

I could imagine the baseball talk going on in the car behind me. Adam's team had won our town's world series just before we left, and I could almost hear Mike and Adam dissecting every play of the season.

# 8

## *RIGHT TURN AT THE PACIFIC: Oregon, Idaho*

At the state line, where we stopped to take a "Welcome To Oregon" picture, Funky Bicycle Man, dressed in camouflage from head to toe, pedaled down into California. Strapped to the back of his bike was a huge box-on-wheels, painted in camouflage, and, presumably, containing all his worldly possessions. His dog, also a character, sat on top of the box. If the dog had worn a scarf and leather helmet, he would have been a body double for Snoopy piloting his doghouse, ready to shoot the Red Baron out of the sky. Up here in the mist and fog, people, and dogs, were individuals.

After Brookings, the full splendor of the Oregon coast took over. We rode past and onto soaring cliffs that rose straight and massive out of the surf. Offshore rock formations loomed like titanic hulls of sinking ships. There was nothing between us and the rocks and dunes and sea as we climbed up Oregon on Route 101.

RV parks and boat harbors peppered the populated parts of the coast, and old men fished for crabs, using bait smashed between pieces of screen tied to the end of a string. Trucks loaded with fresh-cut redwood and cedar logs plied the curving coastal road on their way to Oregon and California mills where cut boards sat stacked six feet high behind metal fences.

Port Orford's elementary school was called Driftwood, and the town recycling station had bins for "Junk Mail." We got coffee at the Wheelhouse Restaurant and stuck a pin in Massachusetts. In 2001, 3,080 American and Canadian visitors had stuck pins in the Wheelhouse map to show where they came from. The restaurant lumped all other pin-stickers into a category called "The World," and, in 2001, 348 of them had bought pancakes or French toast at the Wheelhouse and left their marks on the map.

Who was the visitor from Greenland, I wondered, and what had brought him or her to Oregon? Vacation? Relatives? Research on seals, fog, fishing? What route, air and land, had this person taken between Greenland and Oregon? The act of travel is, itself, intriguing. The pin stuck in Greenland was a wonderful question mark.

Port Orford's fishing harbor was completely fogbound, and we could see only the bottom reaches of the spectacular monolith that towered over the port. Some boats were for sale. A bumper sticker on a pickup read, "Work Harder – Millions on Welfare Depend on You."

Oregon is the land of Drive-Thru Espresso, and we'd meet these ubiquitous, usually homemade-looking kiosks from one end of the state to the other, in cities and towns, and in tiny, remote, unlikely places. People sold Drive-Thru Espresso from plywood A-frames, slapdash shacks, and trailers sitting in the corners and middles of parking lots and on dirt pullouts off the road. Gas stations offered fuel for vehicles and drive-thru caffeine for their occupants. Sportsmen's centers sold bait, tackle and Drive-Thru Espresso. A Chemult shop advertised "Gourmet Espresso, Hot Mamas and Road Munchies." (I have no idea.) Even tiny Mitchell, which sits in lonely brown mountains near a memorial to frontier Mail Carrier H.H. Wheeler, attacked by Indians in 1888, had its kiosk: "Get Your Fix at Route 26 Espresso."

At Florence, we turned east. We were 5,000 miles and a continent from it, but we were pointed toward home. Mike had only just started his journey, and would end it in Montana in a week, so, for him the right turn at the Pacific meant something because it meant something to us. Mike's investment in the turn east and the family that made it yielded him a moment of sweet vicariousness as he watched us beam and giggle. Here were his kids, in Florence, Oregon, about to start their return trip across a continent.

For Adam, Dana and I, the turn onto Route 126 – Route 126 *east* – was a special moment. I suspect New Paint felt it, too. I imagined her feeling proud at having served us so well and resolving to do the same in the second half.

The turn away from the ocean put us back into wildfire country. The Eugene *Register-Guard's* front page listed twelve "hot spots" between us and Idaho. We savored the views of the snowy Cascades as we neared Bend, knowing the cool iciness would be memory once we stepped off into the high, dry Oregon desert. Near Gilchrist, "Home of the Grizzlies," 93.7 FM gave a weather report: "A little smoky out there. Stay by the pool."

Fire has shaped this landscape for eons. Newberry Volcanic Monument sat 13 miles off Route 97 in LaPine. We passed the area's campgrounds, where people had tacked messages written on white paper plates to boards at the camp entrances. We came to the Big Obsidian Flow, a wondrous mountain of sparkling black glass exploded from the earth's core 1,300 years ago.

We climbed nearly a mile up the razor sharp flow, careful to stay on the path so we wouldn't cut our shoes or legs. The jet black obsidian mountain was sprinkled with gray and white pumice, light as balsa wood. We had the translucent silica peak to ourselves, and we marveled at everything in this surprising, otherworldly landscape. Oh, how tempting to put a piece of black volcanic glass in my pocket to sit in the living room with the salty rock from the Dead Sea and the broken mani stone from Tibet and the chunk of polished marble from a Lisbon sidewalk. But removing stones was forbidden, and the rules applied to us even though I wanted to bend down and put a piece of this earth into my pocket and take it home.

The flow was flanked by Paulina and East Lakes. Mt. Bachelor and the Three Sisters, soon to be full in our faces as we neared Bend, sat close by. At the flow's summit, so unlike anything we'd ever seen or stood on, the kids placed gleaming obsidian chunks atop the travelers' cairns that dotted the path. Had we come a month later, we might have seen the thousands of frogs that converge on Big Obsidian in August. They come, experts think, from nearby Lost Lake, and arrange themselves so thickly that hikers often have to walk around or between them. Thank goodness we were a month early. Dana's an animal person, and would have loved to hike a path alive with creatures, but the rest of us prefer our obsidian straight up, no frogs, thank you.

Home in Bend was a $65 two-room motel suite with a full kitchen and the last phone hookup I figured I'd see in a while, so I fired off the next newspaper installment while we were still communicado. We watched the welders slug it out with the guys from the Desert Air Heating & Air Conditioning Company in a men's over-40 softball game in sculptured, green Drake Park. Before we left beautiful Bend in the morning, we listened to the Indian motel owner on the phone trying to wake his help and get them to show up for work.

"Where ya headed today?" asked the gas station attendant.

"Well, from the look of the map on the front page of the *Redmond Bulletin*, we're heading smack into four fires," I said, hoping he'd tell me the story was overblown, journalistic hyperbole.

Instead, he yelled, "Yeah!" and confirmed the blazes' names: Malheur, 747, Monument and Flagtail. "Yeah! Big ones! Oregon's burning! Everything about it is burning!"

He finished the fill-up, told us his roommate was from Boston, grinned gigantically, and waved us off with, "Have a good one!" Driving out, we noticed a sign advertising "Dog Water."

"What is Dog Water?" gushed Dana, alarmed.

"I don't know, Dane. I truly do not know."

We discussed dog water as we drove into Oregon's high desert dust. What, specifically, made dog water different from people water? Was it recycled toilet or dish water? Was it just plain tap water? Could people drink this dog water without getting sick? Was there a dog water bottling plant somewhere? Did the dogs know they were getting, presumably, worse water than their masters? Did their masters know? Did they care? These thoughts occupied our minds, mostly because our minds wanted something to think about other than the Oregon Burning we were apparently driving into.

Chocolate anthills. Cinnamon rises. Brown velvet gumdrops. The fertile cinder cone hummocks of Route 26 gave on to wild canyons and stone mountains near John Day, resting place for thousands of prehistoric fossils that "weather out," become visible, and are then removed to museums for preservation.

We crossed creeks with names like Murderers, Widows and Rattlesnake, the latter still in abundance. After a scream from a woman in the parking lot at the John Day Fossil Beds, a ranger hooked the rattler resting under her Jeep's driver door and put it in the Visitor Center's "Snake Box." Good eyes, lady. I had trouble stepping into or out of New Paint for the next hundred miles.

We got out to stretch near Prairie City and were assaulted by the smell of smoke. Malheur National Forest was on fire. We drove through it, nearly alone, and every dirt road shooting off the paved road we drove on was blocked with a sawhorse and sign warning, "Road Closed To Entry Due To Fire." The campgrounds of Wallowa-Whitman National Forest were open, but abandoned. No one was out here. I felt a pang of guilt at having pulled Mike across the continent so he could use his precious vacation time to drive through suckingly dry wildfire country.

But that's the soul of adventure. The not being able to know or plan everything, or even anything, ahead of time. Taking what the moment serves up and finding something essential. Through the smoke, we appreciated landscape that was, despite the hand of man running his fingers through its forests, rough, and deserving of respect. And now, demanding it.

An entire adhoc firefighting city appeared at Burnt River High School in Unity. This was bigger than the Coleville operation in California. Hundreds of tents lined the school's ball fields. Support systems indicated workers were in for a long stay: All Fired Up Mobile Laundry Service, outhouses, dumpsters, Texaco gasoline tankers, thousands of pounds of boxed food stacked under yellow tarps, a water truck sprinkling a football field so wildcatters could catch a little dust-free recreation, 18-wheelers from several states hauling supplies to and from the fire camp, a hand-painted sandwich board around the corner at Stratton's Store advising, "Gov't. Vehicles Fuel Here."

After Unity, we began to see ranches, their irrigation systems meting out just enough precious water to coax something from the dusty land. Life here was so scorchingly dry I wondered why the shop in tiny Brogan bothered to offer "Hot Soup Buck A Cup." It might appeal in the middle of the night when the sun was down and the desert was cool, but an offer of hot soup as you drove in blistering heat dodging wildfires seemed absurd, even painful. Livestock hay yielded to wheat and corn as we neared Jamieson and Willow Creek, where a sign asked, "Malheur County Fair – Are You Ready?" (Or, might you still need a "4-H Pig Waterer?") Vale, a railhead where we discovered we were riding on part of the Oregon Trail, buzzed with livestock and agricultural operations. Producers Livestock Market, "Sale every Wednesday;" a Purina Grain elevator; mushroom farms; Hawley Meatpacking; an old downtown and an Onion Avenue; men in huge harvesters with air-conditioned cabs cutting wheat and churning up clouds of dust; signs for the "Spanish Sweet Onion Festival;" pickers in conical bamboo hats hunching in the black-dirt rows of onions, the translucent white onion heads poking out of the earth and growing right up to the edges of the shoulderless road.

We crossed the green Snake River and entered Idaho. 5 p.m., 105 degrees. We found a cheap motel room in Boise and crashed.

Boise was a hundred degree high altitude mellow street party at its old downtown core near the state capitol. A very cool hot place. Kids splashed in the fountains and parents drank cold beers in the "Alive After Five" fest in a plaza between some tall office buildings. The Basque neighborhoods were alive with al fresco diners. We ate at Mohsen "Max" Mohammadi's Casbah. Max was proud of both Boise ("To you, Boise must seem just like a big neighborhood, but it is a very good place.") and the letter he'd received that day from AAA awarding him three diamonds in next year's tour guide.

In about two weeks, I'd start marathon training in earnest, so I had to start tucking some miles under my shoes. A 6 a.m. downtown Boise run, my first since the cautious Tahoe miles, refueled my love for these early runs. The miles were tough, as my muscles hadn't run in nearly nine months, and we were at altitude. My lungs and legs screamed.

But, how wonderful to watch a place wake up. I saw Boise shake the sleep from its eyes. I saw the early risers pull in to sit at formica breakfast counters. I saw the red clouds of sunrise wrap around the high white dome of the capitol. I saw nurses and staff of St. Luke's Hospital park their cars and make their way to work in the cresting heat of morning, donuts and coffee in hand. I saw Boise men in lightweight khakis and tie-less short-sleeve print shirts walk to their offices. Had their pants been shorter, we might have been in Bermuda. Boise going to work looked as mellow as last night's Boise wrapping up after a work day. It seemed a content, healthy place to live. First impressions last, and Boise's were good ones. You have to love a place with enough self-confidence to go tie-less when it's hot.

We met Mackie at the Sinclair station in Idaho City, full of gold boom era buildings on the National Register of Historic Places and the smell of morning bacon and eggs cooking at Calamity Jane's and The Shady Lady. Mackie's tan, thin face radiated below the brim of his farm cap. "Yer all a long way from home," he said, after he'd finished pumping. "How do you like the west?"

We loved it, we enthused, "except for the fires, which you can keep." Mackie told us Idaho was different, because the state used controlled burns, dropping accelerator from planes in containers that looked like ping pong balls. "But, we had 600 lightning strikes on Monday, so they're on the way," he said, of the wildfires that even Idaho probably wouldn't escape.

Mackie loved Idaho and wouldn't be anywhere else. On the day we met him, he was on his way to Challis, a hundred mountain miles away, to see if a mine would hire him on. If he found a job, he'd live in Challis for as long as the work held out. Mackie's permanent home was "on the budget side" of More's Creek Canyon, stunning and deep, with a wide river threading its bottom. On one side of the canyon lay homes of the well-to-do, high above the river on the rim of the canyon wall. On Mackie's side, the setting was less dramatic, and the price of entry less dear.

Mackie said that, on his side, "most of us are in manufacturing." He was a sheetmetal worker.

Although his family tree had roots there, Mackie had "always felt sorry for people back east" (for the simple reason, I'd soon conclude, that they weren't in Idaho). His dad, from Poughkeepsie, New York, graduated from Harvard Medical School and went west to become "one of three or four surgeons" in Idaho Falls. He hadn't necessarily intended to stay, but he met Mackie's mom. "A redhead," said Mackie with a twinkle, as if that were all he needed to say about the eastern doctor's decision to make the move permanent.

That's how Mackie came to belong to Idaho, and he thanked the stars. If he had to work a spell in faraway Challis, that was okay. He'd still wake each day in the Idaho mountains he loved and knew intimately. And he'd have to check in on his dad, then 89 and still living in Idaho Falls.

Later that day, I read a story in the *Idaho Statesman* about the Dow's most recent tailspin. The reporter had asked 28-year-old Pim Hayden how she planned to weather the financial storm. "With mutual funds, you can't go wrong," she was quoted as saying. "You can buy something, then go fishing." Pim's Idahoan outlook reminded me of Mackie.


"The Sawtooth'll knock you out," Mackie had said. At Flat Creek, the glorious massiveness of the whole range spread beside us. Galena Summit, queen of the Sawtooth at 8,701 feet, dominated the center of this majestic set of alpine teeth poised to bite the sky.

In Stanley, built of logs and home to one hundred permanent souls, we sipped Moose Drool at Sawtooth Luce's (the waitress unable to render opinion on the beer's taste because she didn't drink) and savored the full-in-your-face view of the range.

The Stanley Community Center doubled as a tourist bureau, and most conversations, brochures and bulletin board notices were about how to find a piece of this outdoor paradise to call your own, either temporarily or longer. We eavesdropped on conversations and heard the Stanley staffers give retired couples inside information on places to rent or buy or "guys to get in touch with."

Our tent fit three, and we had four, a fact I started to contemplate shortly after we drove through and nodded at tony Ketchum and Sun Valley and satellites Hailey and Bellevue. No celebrities out on the sidewalks. Here, the mountains ended, and the high desert began. These places looked too expensive to overnight in, so, unless we found a cheap motel in a desert town, it looked like we'd be camping.

At tiny Carey, we realized there'd be no motels at all until Arco ("FIRST CITY IN THE WORLD TO BE LIT BY ATOMIC POWER"), long past where I wanted to end the day's driving. The school in Carey had a sign announcing next fall's new teacher: "Welcome Mr. Pinock – Music." Had Mr. Pinock seen Carey, I wondered, before accepting the job? Did he know it was a few storefronts sitting in flat, 5,000-foot dustiness? Would he live in Stanley (swelling its population to a hundred and one) or Arco, and commute daily over great, dry distances to teach music in Carey? Or would he live in town, where he'd bump into his students and their parents and his school colleagues at every turn? I wonder if Mr. Pinock is still there, teaching music in Carey, Idaho.

Later, I tried to call my dad to wish him a happy 71st birthday, but there was no cell reception on the moon. We'd set up housekeeping at Craters of the Moon, a volcanic wonderland. The gate ranger was so thrilled to see my Golden Eagle Passport

("Have you gotten good use of it?" "7,000 miles worth!"), that she gave us the inside scoop on the monument's best tent sites. Number 30 was primo, and we nabbed it.

Actually, a couple from Kentucky ceded it to us. They were sitting on the site's picnic table, looking out over the lava field of *pahoehoe* and *aa*. They had no tent, no trailer, no unpacked gear. They were just enjoying. But dusk was around the corner, and we'd entered those hours when the hunt for somewhere to sleep took on an urgent edge. Anyone still on the road who didn't plan to drive through to the Tetons or west to Ketchum would soon be here, prowling for a little piece of pumice paradise to pitch their tent or park their pop-up. I wanted site 30. The Kentuckians were gracious and understanding when I drove up and gave them a "So, you stayin' or goin'?" look. "We're just hanging out," they said, getting up and smoothing their clothes. "You can have the site. But not next year!" A reconnaissance mission. They pulled out. We pulled in.

The site was set high over the spectacular North Crater lava field in a cul-de-sac of three or four sites. I spread our chairs and tables and tent and van as far across our own huge site as I could to make the cul-de-sac look well-occupied. A blue Saab sniffed around for a while, but I didn't act welcoming, and they went elsewhere. I'd created the illusion that the whole cul-de-sac was ours, and everyone who drove by looking for a site kept going. We ended the evening with no neighbors. Just a quarter acre of pumice and lava and one of the only trees in this eerily beautiful moonscape.

The kids ran and wandered and explored. Dana and Mike took a sundown walk through the North Crater field, Dana stooping down with her little camera to take close-ups of the patterns the cooled lava had settled into thousands of years before. Adam sat under the tree on a cinder and ash rise and surveyed the scene and played with his Gameboy. Dana built jumps from piles of pumice and decorated them with pine cones, then bounded over them like a show horse. Adam took batting practice, hitting Mike's pitches of pumice to Dana in the lava outfield. I sat in the 85-degree late evening heat with my journal, writing about what they were doing, and thinking up fake magazine article titles: "101 Fun Volcanic Activities," "50 Ways to Love Your Lava."

God got me back for commandeering the whole cul-de-sac. I was not one of the three people in our three-person tent. I spent a wicked night in the van, legs bent, hips sore, freezing in shorts and no socks, with just a sheet as cover. I couldn't make a dead-of-night ruckus in the silent, sleeping campground to ferret out warmer gear, so I suffered through. I hoped the kids were warm enough.

The good part was that I didn't sleep at all, and so, witnessed the fantastic heat lightning show that blazed all night over the eastern Idaho desert and danced with the full moon.

I ran the North Crater lava trail at 6:30 the next morning. The moon was still up. As I ran through the surreal flow, the sun worked its way upward and turned the surrounding ancient craters a burnt red-green, a color I'd never seen. Then, the moon and sun met in the sky and faced each other across the lava field. I imagined their conversation, the sun saying, "You go rest. I'll take over now."

## 9

## *MOUNTAINS: Northwest Wyoming, Montana*

To get from the moon to Wyoming, we passed through two worlds, one unsettling, the other soothing.

At the Big Lost River rest area in Idaho's high desert, Department of Energy placards outside the bathrooms tried to make us believe that this sagebrush expanse, realm of Idaho National Engineering and Environmental Laboratory (INEEL), a totally nuclear world, was also a wildlife preserve. Thank goodness for this wilderness where scientists could study bobcats, coyotes and pronghorn.

We were primed for something to spice up this long, dry ride, and here it was. "Ahhh, yes, one of our favorite stops on the whole trip was the INEEL wildlife preserve!" We joked that any wildlife studies, whose existence we doubted, wouldn't be about pronghorn per se, but about how many extra horns pronghorn grew after living in this nuclear wasteland.

Two suspicious men in the rest area parking lot heightened the fun and intrigue. They were traveling separately, in nondescript sedans, and stared at us from behind sunglasses. They read the exhibit information as if they were interested, trying to act like tourists. They didn't fool us. They weren't here to stretch their legs or learn about bobcats. We pegged them as FBI or CIA, protecting eastern Idaho's reactors and nuclear detritus from terrorists, or keeping an eye on activists and celebrity landowners who objected to INEEL's plan to burn waste contaminated with plutonium.

On top, the land looked dead, dry, innocuous. Below was a honeycomb of stuff we just wanted to drive over and get away from. INEEL stores high-level nuclear waste. Spent naval and nuclear reactor fuel. Surplus plutonium. We imagined what was going on in tunnels under us. We hummed the "doo-DOO-doo-DOO" theme from "The Twilight Zone."

Radar apparatus, satellite towers and huge communication systems festooned the tops of buttes. No ranches, livestock or towns. Yellow school buses plied dirt roads that shot off the highway. They brought workers to sites like Argonne West. There were scores of reactors out there in the desert, about 50 over a 900-square mile expanse. We turned up the driveway of EBR-1, the "World's First Nuclear Power Plant and National Historic Landmark, Open Daily from 9-5, Free to the Public." Adam wanted to tour it, but was voted down three to one. The rest of us found it eerie, looming there at the end of the access road. And nobody was out here but us (and the G-men), making it even creepier.

I made a mental note to try never to get a potato that had spent time in one of the steel Quonset huts or long triangular barns of sod and dirt that lined the highway just east of INEEL. "Hot potatoes," one of us jeered. Hard to drive through this nuclear desert and then order some fries or a nice big baked with your entrée. I developed temporary potatophobia in eastern Idaho, one of the planet's several potato capitals.

In the Conant Valley nearer Wyoming, things turned lush and alive. For single ladies, there may be no better place in the US to see beautiful men than Swan Valley, Idaho, on the South Fork of the Snake River. The Snake here is liquid art. Broad and bending, light sage green, it rushes with small white water, and drifts in silvery ripples. Fingers of treed islands and peninsulas cut and divide it, and wader-clad flyfishermen cast their arcing lines into its flow, lit by a movie set sun.

Swan Valley's population is 260, and it seemed to me a good percentage of that number are fit, gorgeous men, many young, many blond, all quite stupendous. Sit a spell in South Fork Outfitters (where fish-shaped bottles hold the bathroom soap, and a poster above the sink reads, "For Those Who Appreciate the Finer Things in Life, Like Hands That Smell of Fish"). Pick yourself out a fetching pair of hipwaders. But, before you cast your line, for fish or man, you'd better know your way around a driftboat and how to tie a damn good fly, because these boys aren't about looking pretty. They're about serious flyfishing. Looky-loos and dilettantes might earn five polite minutes of their time.

A storm gathered as we neared the Tetons. I didn't want to stay in Jackson, but after we drove through it and entered Teton National Park, Mike called all the park lodges. Booked solid. It was early afternoon. A few park campgrounds had open sites, but the thunderheads sitting on Grand Teton and Mt. Owen told us camping wasn't a good idea. We turned around. By three in the afternoon, a mile-long backup of would-be National Parkers lined the road back into Jackson, trying to find a roof for the night against the now driving rain. We'd beat them back in by a hair and had nabbed one of the last rooms in town.

Jackson isn't the kind of place we relate to. Families drop big bucks for breakfast. If you've no dinner reservation at one of the popular restaurants, you might be eating a granola bar on a street corner, as there's precious little casual, reasonably priced middle ground. Blocks of boutiques sell useless, expensive things to people whose closest encounter with the mountains are the silkscreened scenes on their thirty-dollar t-shirts. We tried to find something real in Jackson. Like a piece of fruit.

A conversation with a cashier confirmed that the town holds travelers hostage in restaurants and tourist establishments, vacuuming up their cash. I went looking for fresh food, but, in all the blocks of downtown Jackson, found only souvenir and clothing shops. In a postcard-cum-convenience store, where I scored milk and orange juice, I asked the cashier where I could buy some produce.

"The closest place is a mile out of town."

"You mean you have to drive a mile out of Jackson to buy fresh fruit and vegetables?" I asked, amazed.

"Yup," said the cashier, and lowered her eyes.

We connected in a silent way over the absurd absence of fresh produce in a town like Jackson, writ big on the map. She didn't like it, either.

I ran Jackson at 6:30 the next morning. Forty-seven degrees. Hat, gloves, labored breath hanging like a cloud. I felt the altitude, and the run was work. In the parking lot of the Snow King Ski Area, float trippers were getting on school buses for the ride to their entry point on the Snake River. Some of them were woefully underdressed, and I lobbed a mental wish in their direction that God would get the sun up and out faster today to warm these poor shiverers about to get into an open raft in sub-50 temps to ride a cold river.

I ran Jackson from one corner to another, and, besides the shops, restaurants and motels that catered to the tourist trade, I saw three dominant types of business in town: real estate offices, appraisers, and lawyers. On the street the night before, I'd overheard two men chatting about a common acquaintance:

"Do you know her?"

Yeah! I sold her a condo…"

Before we left Jackson for the now rain-free and gloriously purple Tetons, we stopped at the Saturday morning farmer's market on the town's central square (in whose middle sits a park with arched entrances built from shed elk antlers collected by the Boy Scouts). We bought gorgeous produce at excellent prices from farmers who come down from the surrounding mountains to service the residents of Jackson. Tourists were still in bed, or eating six dollar restaurant eggs.

But, someone has to make sure the people who run this western theme town have something fresh and reasonably priced to eat. Mike heard one young woman, paper sack of good bounty in hand, thank the farmer she'd bought from for "continuing to come down." Just one of the many Jackson workers who can't afford six dollar eggs and hope the mountain farmers keep coming to the valley on Saturday mornings.

The red and purple splendor of Teton National Park lies just beyond Jackson, and when we came to the Tetons, an exquisite all-in-one-eyeful mountain world, I appreciated Jackson's role in keeping this place pristine. I saw the symbiosis between the National Park Service and the Jackson-like towns that surround the nation's protected wild places. Travelers can fill up on kitsch and amenities just outside the parks. Then, sated, they can plunge into the natural world, taking it at their own speed. From tame and drive-through to as unplugged and backcountry as they want to be.

There are moments, so many of them as you travel America, when something about this land takes your breath away. Its diversity and beauty enrich and amaze. A gorgeous land, one tableau melting into another. You need only crest the next summit or round the next lake or cross the next valley to come to someplace breathtaking, alive, proud, or peaceful. Someplace vast, productive, interesting, or important.

Often on this journey, when we came to a place that was exquisite in its way, I thought about September 11. On many a 300-mile day, which might have seen us rise in one time zone and retire in another, I thought about terrorism, still jarringly fresh and disturbingly fearsome.

But the magnificence and seeming infiniteness of the land put terrorism into perspective, and I was quieted. I shared my thoughts with Adam and Dana. They would inherit the world we lived in and helped create, and it was important to talk about America not just as a landscape or road trip or series of historic, cultural or scenic stops, but as a living, organic nation of people trying to find its best fit in the puzzle of the world. In trying, we've made and will make mistakes, and, more now than in the past, the world will ask us to pay for them. Sometimes, payment exacted will be fair and just. Sometimes, as on September 11, it will be insane, brutal, and murderous.

But, being out in America, getting up every day with the sun to follow new roads, I fell in love with the country I'd lived in and taken for granted for 44 years. I saw her strength and her strengths. Terrorism would be a fact of life, perhaps for generations, but the country we were traveling through told us not to fear. On the whole, we'll be okay, it said.

America in its soul is a good, honest place. I found myself thinking that terrorists could pick away at small bits of us, like they did in Manhattan, killing people and creating hell on earth in some targeted corner of our world. But they could never take it all down. They could obliterate small pieces and make despair and chaos rain down on some chosen area. But the whole is just too big to bring down, and the people too resolved and resilient. They can't really get us, I'd think, as we drove through endless landscape that changed and changed and brought more wonder the longer you spent in it. They could jab, but the nation's sheer size would keep it standing, with tough pockets and corners stepping in to help tend wounds and fill gaps.

The quiet places intrigued me most. America is not just New York or Chicago or San Francisco or Miami. It's a powerful chain of strong, silent, little known places that relish their freedom and react when it's challenged, whether by bureaucrats, developers, punks, or terrorists. People and places that step in and act when something they love is messed with. I thought and felt this as we moved through the land.

In the Tetons, we stayed in a tent cabin at Coulter Bay, where deer visited our concrete patio. We kept wood in the stove to stave off July's 35-degree nights, and Mounts Moran and Grand Teton basked in yellow, orange, pink or red light, depending on the time of day.

When I was young, I saw a photo in *National Geographic* of two women with big beehive hair and black horn-rimmed glasses sitting on a bench in the great common room of Jackson Lake Lodge. They sat in front of the floor to ceiling windows and looked out at the Tetons. I've wanted to see the Tetons ever since. And, I've wanted to see them from that room, on that bench.

We left our tent cabin for a few hours and sat in the great room at Jackson Lake Lodge. I sat on the bench.

The great, high-ceilinged room is filled with couches and chairs upholstered in cinnamon, tan and hunter green. Western hues. Families play Monopoly or cards, and people read and drink wine and look out the wall of windows to a mountain range of staggering beauty. I've seen higher, wilder, more exotic mountains, but none more exquisite than the Tetons.

When I was planning this trip, my father told me the Tetons were my Uncle Ed's favorite place on earth. When I was in my twenties, Uncle Ed and Aunt Lil sold their house outside Burlington, Vermont in the hug of the Green Mountains, and went to live on the Atlantic and Caribbean in their sailboat. But even with that casting off from terra firma, I always thought of them as Vermonters, not explorers, and never knew my uncle had been to the Tetons. When I saw these snow-covered stone beauties, I thought of my Uncle Ed. He knew his mountains.

Adam bought playing cards at the gift shop, and we sat on sofas and listened to a young woman play classical music on the Boston grand piano near the bar. The pianist wore jeans and a brown shirt, and she'd thrown her backpack into one corner near the piano, her coat in another, as if she couldn't wait to open the keyboard cover and start moving her fingers. She loved to play. Whenever I took my eyes from the mountains and looked over at her, playing rich 18th and 19th century compositions, she was smiling at the music. Many of us clapped after the pieces, and she graciously acknowledged the applause. But I could tell she would have been just as happy had she and the piano been there alone.

The Tetons melt into Yellowstone. We were at about 8,000 feet and crossed the Continental Divide three times. Yellowstone was wild, foggy, immense, and full of bison and steaming earth.

"You traveling?" I asked the young guy sitting next to us in Gardiner, Montana's Yellowstone Mine restaurant. To get to Gardiner, where the Yellowstone River rushes through the center of town, we drove through the Roosevelt Arch at Yellowstone's North Entrance on the Wyoming-Montana border. In a 1903 speech, Teddy Roosevelt had dedicated the dark stone arch, saying, "The Yellowstone Park is something absolutely unique in the world…This Park was created and is now administered for the benefit and enjoyment of the people…It is the property of Uncle Sam and therefore of us all." "FOR THE BENEFIT AND ENJOYMENT OF THE PEOPLE" is chiseled across the top of this first gateway to the world's first national park. Yellowstone was the first place on earth to celebrate democracy by setting aside land to be kept free from settlement or development.

We'd driven down into Montana for dinner from our Mammoth Hot Springs hotel, which sat five miles away from Gardiner.

Five miles of such astonishing mountain beauty it was impossible to keep driving. I pulled off the road at the Lava Creek Trailhead, which overlooked a soul-stirring panorama, a view that reached wide and deep and long into both Montana and Wyoming. Montana stretched away in undulations of burnt-gold velvet mountains, hummocks carpeted in rich sienna pile, smooth and treeless, shaped like great, soft-furred bison sleeping under the pink evening sky. I sat on a rock and let the velvet bison and the pink sky become part of me, while Mike and the kids bounded down the steep Lava Creek Trail. They reached the creek bed, hundreds of feet below where I sat on my rock, and they ran alongside the green, rushing water. They became specks, but the wind kept us connected. It carried their voices up the mountainside to my rock, so I could listen to their joy.

Gambling being legal in Montana, Yellowstone Mine had a small casino in the bar next to the main dining room, and Dana kept getting up from the table to stand in the casino doorway, careful not to cross the line. The bar stools were built like the hindquarters of horses. Dana would eat a few forkfuls, then go look at the line of horses waiting at the bar for a drink. People sat in some of the stools, and from the back, they looked like they were chatting with the bartender from a saddle atop a horse.

The diner next to us beamed as he answered my question about his presumed status as a road warrior. " I'm seven days into a sixteen-day trip." He was from Ohio, traveling alone, loving every second. "You?"

"About five weeks into a seven-week trip."

He whistled appreciatively. We all tucked into our food (my garlic parmesan soup was to die for, but when I said as much to the waitress, she told me to head to 4-B's in Bozeman if I wanted really outrageous soup. "It's a drive, and my boyfriend hates it, but they have the best tomato soup! Whenever I go away, the first thing I do is go to 4-B's for the tomato soup!").

I turned back to the guy from Ohio, who was relishing his beer and every bite of his meal. He was treating himself. A break from cans or fast food or something cold from a convenience store. The slow, satisfied feeling of sitting awhile in a good environment enjoying hot food. Maybe he was rewarding himself for crossing a whole state or two today. He was clearly happy.

"It's fun, isn't it." I said it as a statement, not a question. He grinned big.

"Yeah, I love living out of a suitcase."

"Me too. Only with the family, I'm living out of a tailgate."

Suitcase or tailgate, we agreed being on the road was a gift.

I loved meeting people hardwired with wanderlust. I thought of Jeff, a boy we'd met at Citizen's Harbor in Crescent City, California. We were on the pier, looking at the old fishing boats and piles of crab pots, when a gleaming mahogany kayak sliced through the water and came to rest just below us. The boat was a work of art, so we were curious about who was in it. Up the pier's ladder climbed Cliff from Chico, California, his son Jeff, and nephew, Michael. Every summer they camp with their extended family in the redwoods near Crescent City and ocean kayak in one of the four exquisite wooden craft handmade by Cliff's dad. Cliff was a worldly, well-traveled man, and we talked of many places. Jeff, no more than 14, was an articulate participant in the conversation. I asked him if he'd also been to all the places we'd talked about. "No," he said. "I like maps." I saw myself at 14 and bet Jeff would take places on maps and turn them into rich experiences and memories as he moved through his life.

We made our way slowly out of Yellowstone, drinking in the powerful beauty of this immense wild place, and headed for the Northeast Entrance, which would deliver us into Montana. As we drove through Lamar Valley, site of the National Park Service's Buffalo Ranch, we saw large herds of bison, and one small herd of nine ladies from Denver who were about to embark on a five-day pack trip across the valley. The ladies, experienced riders all, had one fear: buffalo. They should have been underway already, but something literally sat in their way. I talked to the woman who'd lassoed her friends into this trip. (She'd heard about the pack tours "at the Future Farmers of America convention.") She sat on her horse, ready to ride into the wilderness, but was afraid of just one thing: "The buffalo sittin' straight out there."

Smart to be scared. Mike and Dana had taken a trail ride from the stables near Mammoth Hot Springs and had talked a lot about the viciousness of bison and the stupidity of tourists with Justin and Erin, their wrangler and wrangler-in-training. Bison were the only animals Justin was afraid of. Every morning before starting the day's rides, the stable sends scouts onto the trails to look for buffalo. Justin talked about the tourists who die every year from bison attacks. When we drove into Yellowstone, the ranger who checked my Golden Eagle Passport had handed us a flyer. It said to keep away from the bison, and told of the non-heeders gored and killed each year. One man tried to put his three-year-old daughter atop a buffalo for a photo. The man is dead. From Yellowstone on into Custer State Park in South Dakota, we'd see people, out of their cars, cameras poised, walking close to these wild, horned behemoths, cooing to them as if they were puppies.

As we rode through this wild country, I noticed that the middle finger of my left hand, which takes most of the steering wheel pressure, was completely callused. My trophy for nearly 8,000 miles of driving.

The Beartooth Parkway, one of the planet's most spectacular ribbons of high altitude asphalt, snaked us through the Rockies, delivering us from Wyoming to Montana. Mountains embraced us on all sides, and the road rose and twisted and switchbacked its way up through the Shoshone and Custer National Forests to the sky, taking us with it, keeping us for hours at between eight and eleven thousand feet. We reached the snow line and made summer snowballs. On this day, the drive itself, 127 miles over five and a half hours, was the day's main event.

Adam and Dana appreciated the scenery between videos. They watched a *Dinosaurs* movie (a family of reptilian Simpsons) called *The Last Temptation of Ethyl*. Grandma Ethyl, claiming a personal connection with muckety-mucks in the hereafter, cons people into paying her to reserve them a spot in heaven before it fills up. She becomes a televangelist. For a good third of the Beartooth ride, the back seats sang, to the tune of "Swing Low, Sweet Chariot," a song that urged grandma's viewers to not only give dough to the Ethyl Show, but to give enough to carry them home.

Déjà vu (actually deja entendu). There is, apparently, something about glorious mountain roads through snow-capped peaks that induces my children to sing silly songs, ad nauseum and ad infinitum. "Jingle Bells, Batman smells..." in the Pyrenees. "Give dough..." in the Rockies. Maybe it's oxygen depletion.

It was on the Beartooth that we really started to see the bikers. We joined a group of Harley pilots on the front porch of Top of the World Store & Motel ("Population 6" - the Milam family). Inside, the family was doing a brisk business in soda, snacks and t-shirts.

The bikers were headed for South Dakota and the mother of all motorcycle rallies, Sturgis Bike Week. The Doobie Brothers and Nitty Gritty Dirt Band would headline. From the Beartooth to the Great Lakes, we'd share highways, byways, gas stations, campgrounds, rest areas and tourist sites with bikers from all over America. Under their leather jackets they packed Nikons and Minoltas, and they stopped at the same scenic overlooks and beauty spots as the rest of us.

They provided Adam with a five-state rolling smorgasbord of chrome and parts, gadgets and detailing, spokes and sidecars. I was nervous, telling him not to get too close to the parked machines. There were so many of them lined up everywhere we stopped that if one went down, it would take at least a dozen with it. I had nightmares of having to pay for a mass of toppled, bruised Harleys because I was the mother of the kid who'd set the domino line in motion. I respected their outrageous expensiveness by parking far away and making a wide arc around them as I walked to the bathroom or coffee machine or gift shop.

At Silver Gate, Montana, full of rustic cabins and flyfishing outfitters, we saw we were following part of the Nez Perce Trail. I told the kids what I knew of Chief Joseph and the relentless push of white men west. For 108 days in 1877, Chief Joseph led his people away from an aggressively advancing U.S. Army. The Nez Perce fought while they made their retreat, but were greatly outnumbered, sick, and starving. His tribe decimated, Chief Joseph surrendered at Bears Paw Mountain in Montana, not far from where we stood by the side of the road in Silver Gate, speaking the grief-filled words, "My heart is sick and sad. From where the sun now stands I will fight no more forever."

Dana bought a book about the Nez Perce at our next stop. It was fiction, and horses played a big part in the story and cover art, but she probably wouldn't have bought it had she not traveled the Beartooth and read the Nez Perce story on the wooden sign by the side of the road in Silver Gate, Montana.

We were on our eventual way to Billings, where we'd drop Mike to catch his plane home. We'd miss him, and he'd miss us even more because he'd be alone, and it got harder to get closer to

Billings. He'd be flying out on his birthday, so we wanted to make the last night of his trip special. My Nevada gas station near-disaster notwithstanding, I have pretty good map sense. I'd had a feeling about Red Lodge, Montana and had picked it as our pre-Billings overnight stop. We needed a good place to celebrate Mike's 45th birthday and his part in our journey across America.

Red Lodge, named for the color the Crow painted their meeting houses, is an old coal mining town on Rock Creek that has morphed into a successful travel destination, especially in winter when the town's ski mountain is packed with powder. For us, Red Lodge is a great family memory. When Mike wears the t-shirt from Bogart's, a Mexican restaurant filled with nice people and mounted deer heads, where we ate our birthday cum farewell dinner, we smile and remember. "Bogart's. Established 1975. Red Lodge, Montana." Like all the t-shirts in the world that people buy because they confirm something good or important in their lives – a place, a race, a team, a school, a company, a cause – the Red Lodge shirt makes good memories every time it's worn.

We scouted the town and settled on the Chateau Rouge because it had an indoor pool. What we got for our $89 was a two-story, two-bedroom slice of mountain heaven with a kitchen, patio, backyard, fireplace, and two TV's, which kept the kids from fighting over the remote, itself worth $89.

While Mike let the kids run wild through the Candy Emporium, I shot pictures of Red Lodge's 19th century brick building fronts, shining crimson and gold in the early evening sun. We cruised Main Street, Dana and Adam hauling candy sacks so full you just had to shake your head. They couldn't talk. Their teeth were stuck together. They'd both be getting braces after we got home, so this was their last stand.

I pointed at the old Pollard Hotel. "Look! Buffalo Bill, Calamity Jane, and William Cullen Bryant stayed here!" Dana stopped chewing long enough to ponder Bill and Jane because she knew they both rode horses, but Bryant drew a "William Cullen who?"

"A poet. From Massachusetts and New York City. 'Thanatopsis?' 'To A Waterfowl?' You guys read any poetry in school? I hated 'Thanatopsis,' but I loved saying the word! Just listen to it: 'Thanatopsis, Thanatopsis, Thanatopsis!'"

Their licorice and jawbreaker-induced stares made me imagine them pushing my wheelchair to the window to see the pretty flowers, patting me on the head, and saying, "See you next week, mom."

We headed toward Billings and goodbyes. The thought of goodbye was sad, but we knew having a goodbye at all meant you'd had time together in the first place. We'd shared 10 good road days. We'd shared stories, campfires and moments of wonder, beauty and learning. We'd felt the pulse of good American places and people.

And, we'd done our normal family things, like telling the kids to stop arguing, mandating they order juice instead of soda before capitulating at their pleas for Sprite and Pepsi, and asking Adam to speak clearly so we could understand him. We'd all had a different take on what we did and saw. We learned to accommodate each other. Mike and the kids (especially the kids) forgave me for getting them out of bed and on the road so early, and for trying to teach them something everywhere we went. We forgave Mike for not putting things back where they'd been and belonged, things that had been so perfectly stowed for the thousands of miles before he joined us. We understood when Adam preferred an Outkast CD to the splendor of the Cascades or thought a video arcade the highlight of the day. We wondered at Dana, who could sniff out or recognize anything even remotely horse-related from miles away.

We had ourselves a time, got to know our country and its people, laughed, relaxed, overcame annoyance and frustration, and sewed ourselves into a tighter-knit family than when we left. We knew we were making good memories, but we also respected that the memories would be different for all of us.

How we chose to record and document the trip differed, too, and told something about each of us. In descending order of amount of recording done and time spent doing it, our family scale went (as it does on every trip) "Mom, Dana, Adam, Dad," with me documenting absolutely everything and Mike absolutely nothing.

I keep journals and shoot hundreds of slides. My Nikon is either on or near me, except when I'm sleeping (actually, it's near me even then, in case I wake up to an incredible play of 5 a.m. light that must be recorded. The family has learned to sleep through the clicking.)

And, I always have paper, often little loose pieces, on which I jot words and phrases, fragments and feelings, facts and quotes, all day long. I number the sheets, then spend every evening turning all the jots into the day's journal entry, sometimes writing for hours. It is a required daily duty, like teeth-brushing, and when circumstances force me to miss a jots-to-journal session, I pour an extra glass of wine the next night and settle in to record not one, but two days. I keep the journals and take the slides because I love doing it, and because I want to be an old woman who can travel back to everywhere all over again by reading the words and looking at the pictures.

There's also a maternal responsibility that pushes me into the role of family record-keeper, preserver, chronicler. My children are world travelers because of me, so I am obliged to document their journeys for them until they're old enough to choose whether and how to record them for themselves. I can't allow what they've seen to slip away from them. They're in these places, all over the globe, because I've taken them there, so I have to provide tools so they can remember. Created from my perspective, surely, but jumping off points, nevertheless.

Dana is a writer, crafting exuberant word pictures that effervesce along the page. She incorporates pieces of what she sees into sweet fiction and occasional poems, and she keeps a sporadic diary, making entries when the mood strikes. (Horse sightings inspire more entries than anything else.)

Dana's journal opens (quite economically – a single paragraph takes us 4,000 miles) with, "From the screaming rides of Hershey Park, to the almost hevenly *(sic)* West Virginia. The soft whinnies of Kentucky, to the wildness of New Orleans and the fresh accents of Tennessee and Texas, we are now in New Mexico, on our way to Colorado. The day is 7/9/02. We pass exquisite mesas, buttes, mounds, and mountains. The sky so blue and gentle, never ends. Little adobe houses are everywhere on the right, as so the left."

On July 14, she wrote: "We drove a long and boring ride in Nevada. Although we did see the carcus *(sic)* of a mustang. On another road we saw another mustang that must have died of heat. Good news! We did see four that were actually alive but, right then I was to *(sic)* sad to really pay attention to them. I had left the ring daddy gave me at the KOA Kabin! I am really having a blakout *(sic)*."

Adam is precise and efficient and has a sharp eye for things that are visually distinctive or intriguing. He doesn't write about his travels. He takes skillful and beautifully dramatic pictures, with little equipment to speak of except his keen eye, shooting with a thirty-five dollar plastic Konica. (I've promised him a good starter 35-mm upon request for any holiday or observance for which we buy gifts. So far, "money" remains his gift of choice, and he continues to coax magnificent pictures from the Konica.)

He also draws quick pencil sketches of things that have lines and corners, interesting shapes and angles. His sketch of Mesa Verde blends the wildfire threat that pervaded the place when we were there with imagined details of life a thousand years ago. In the drawing, sharp, black limbs of burned trees stand behind stacked cliff houses, without people, but with wooden ladders propped at doors and smoke rising from chimneys. His sketch of a two-lane highway, one car traveling in each direction, evokes long, straight, infinite distance. I asked Adam what place he'd depicted. "I don't know. Somewhere."

Yes, it was. His lone farmhouse, set in a vast landscape, empty but for a cow and a few bushes, an unending road leading to distant hills, a crescent of hot sun sitting behind them – was Texas, New Mexico, Colorado, Arizona. Was Utah, Nevada, Oregon. Was Idaho, Wyoming, Montana. Was Somewhere.

Mike carries no camera, notebook, sketchpad, pencils or pens. He is unencumbered by the need, desire or duty to record his journeys. He is content to live and enjoy them in the moment of their taking place, and he derives as much pleasure from being with and watching his family travel as he does from the scenes and places we're traveling in. He knows the journeys are being recorded by the rest of us, so he has nothing to do but be. As I give yet another evening over to the jots-to-journal process, I often envy him having nothing to do. A few times a year he'll ask me a question like, "What was the name of that town in such-and-where with the thus-and-such?" I'll answer, and he'll say, "Oh, yeah. That was a nice place, wasn't it?" All he needs.

As we rolled toward Billings on Route 212, we passed Halvorson Lawn Ornaments in Joliet, which sits on part of the old Bozeman Trail. Mr. Halvorson put his inventory where his mouth is, and hundreds of ornaments, from gnomes to Virgin Marys, were lined up right there on his front lawn. Battalions of them, in parade formation, starting just feet from the bottom step of Halvorson's concrete stoop.

I posed a question-with-answer to my crew. "Where's Halvorson's Lawn Ornaments? On Halvorson's Lawn!" Maybe the cumulative effect of driving 8,500 miles was working its way into my brain cells, but I thought this enormously funny. Had anyone started a chorus of "Give Dough to the Ethyl Show" at that moment, I would have joined in and sung until somebody stopped me. If it hadn't been Halvorson's trolls and birdbaths, it would have been something else, maybe the sign at Kroft's Angus farm proclaiming "Better Bulls." I could have wrung a half-hour of naughty wordplay from that one. I was, temporarily, the long-distance driver equivalent of a punch-drunk boxer.

Long-haul truckers must have moments like this when they, oh, I don't know, try to see how many words they can make from the letters in "Idaho," then "Oregon," then discover that, between the two, they've got id and ego. Or, maybe they get giddy when Petula Clark comes on the radio, and they gear up, singing along slow and sly with the "when you're alone" part, building to the grand, gay "DOWN-town!" which they belt out in a happy, fortissimo shout, maybe with an accompanying arm gesture. Surely, at any given moment, thousands of transcontinental drivers are dealing with symptoms of too-long-behind-the-wheel-itis by engaging in novel examples of brain drivel. If they're riding alone, the cathartic silliness evaporates, unnoticed, into the ether. If they've got passengers, those in shotgun positions may become alarmed, and perhaps suggest a Dairy Queen break.

We crossed the Yellowstone River at hard-working Laurel with its refineries and railheads, and picked up I-90 to Billings. I got a weird sensation when we hit that road. We know I-90. We know it as the Massachusetts Turnpike, the road with the pilgrim hat logo. From here, outside Billings, Montana, it was a straight interstate shot to home. "If we kept going on this road, we'd be on the Mass. Pike," I said. "We could almost beat dad back to Boston. We'd be home the day after tomorrow."

"Let's do it!" shouted Adam, suddenly animated. He knew we wouldn't, but it was worth a try. His friends and endless days of doing nothing and everything were on the other end of this road.

Mike sat back and seemed to envision us in an air-land race, he looking down from a window seat trying to spy New Paint as she raced due east. Dana wasn't enticed by the prospect of a quick exit from this trip. There were still more horses to see.

"We'd miss the Dakotas and the Great Lakes if we bail now," I said, pretending to entertain the idea of interstating it home. "Those are whole chunks of the country that we wouldn't see, that we wouldn't know anything about." Adam, a sharp negotiator who misses no tricks, volleyed with, "We could save them for another trip. It would give us something to see the next time." Very good toss. The kid thinks fast. I applauded his mental agility.

We dropped Mike at his hotel in downtown Billings. I'd booked him something not too far from the airport, but still within reach of things to do on what would likely be a long afternoon and evening. When I saw the women's correctional institution in the neighborhood, I glanced sideways at Mike, hoping he'd missed it.

We went into the lobby to make sure the hotel people hadn't lost his reservation and then went out to the parking lot to say goodbye. We kept it short on purpose. Dana, holding a "Horse Crossing" road sign she'd bought in Red Lodge, posed with her dad for a departure photo. Two waitresses from the inn's restaurant, who were hanging out in a maintenance shed off the parking lot smoking cigarettes, watched our family scene and came out of the shed to clap and wave as we gave final kisses. Adam reclaimed the front seat, and we drove away, leaving Mike alone in a Billings parking lot.

He had a great time in Billings. Went to a book signing in the old Montana Avenue Historic District. Got turned onto the Montana books of Ivan Doig, of which we now have a small collection. Had a few drinks with a sharp, worldly rancher named Jack who knew everything about Montana and thought Ted Turner was a menace because he bought up so much land that he unwittingly killed the downtowns the land was connected to. Mike enjoyed every inch of his time in Billings. I was relieved. I'd been expecting a phone conversation about trying in future to avoid hotels near women's prisons.

Big Horn County was brown, dry, rolling. The Crow Reservation sits on the prairie. At Crow Agency, the reservation's main town, Indians gathered for a festival in a green park off the highway, teepees pitched in the park and pickups lining the perimeter.

When we got to Little Bighorn, I thought of the Crow just down the road, and how they might feel about this national monument. We bought food at the Kentucky Fried Chicken outside the entrance, and I wondered what the young Sioux behind the counter thought of the site that brought in tourists who bought mashed potatoes and popcorn chicken.

I'd seen Little Bighorn many years before from the air, on a flight to somewhere in California. I'd seen Custer's whole hill, and could contemplate the approach, the ambush, the surprise and the death, from 25,000 feet. The sky had been cloudless, as if God had said, "Here, look down now. Look down on a place where men killed each other for reasons even I don't understand."

William Faulkner said, "The past is not dead...it is not even past." Last Stand Hill marks the spots where Custer and some forty of the approximately two hundred and forty Seventh Cavalry soldiers who died on June 25, 1876 fell. Directly across from Last Stand Hill, on the other side of a narrow road, we watched men work, bare-chested in the blast furnace heat, on the Native American monument that will be connected to Last Stand Hill by a rift, a slit, a gash – a physical feature announcing that "a weeping wound or cut exists."

On June 25, 1988, American Indians placed a plaque at the foot of the granite obelisk commemorating Custer and his cavalrymen. Now in the Visitor Center, the plaque holds these words by G. Magpie, Cheyenne: "In honor of our Indian Patriots who fought and defeated the U.S. Calvary *(sic)* In order to save our women and children from mass murder. In doing so, preserving our rights to our Homelands, Treaties, and Sovereignty." At the base of the plaque were items left in tribute: coins, ribbons, flags, and notes saying, "Thank you for honoring the Sioux."

Sioux, Cheyenne and Arapaho fought that day. After the battle, surviving Indians were rounded up and incarcerated, and some who had witnessed the Battle of Little Bighorn drew pictures of what they had seen. Called ledger drawings, they were drawn on the only paper available in military prison camp – ledger paper from the camp commissary. The Marquis and Colter ledger drawing collections hung on the back wall of a Visitor Center room with sweeping views of the battlefield and Last Stand Hill. I turned from the wall to the windows, from the windows back to the wall. Looking at the drawings, – some naïve, some masterfully rendered, all the product of eye, hand, soul and heart – I realized Last Stand was a double-entendre. Yes, it was certainly Custer's, but I was looking at eyewitness accounts of a victory by the victors, who were then swept away to draw pictures on paper that white men used to take stock and make an accurate and precise accounting of things.

## 10

# OPEN SPACES:  Northeast Wyoming, the Dakotas

"Those women are still on that pack trip," mused Dana, after we picked up our cones from the Sheridan, Wyoming Dairy Queen and followed the truck with the "No Subs, No Timeouts, No Wimps- JUST RODEO!" bumper sticker out of the drive-thru, and into Sheridan's historic red brick downtown. I'd thought of the Denver ladies myself once or twice in the last few days and hoped they'd been buffalo-free.

We were back in Wyoming, and the earth was red. Snow fences along I-90, and signs in Buffalo warning "90 CLOSED WHEN FLASHING –RETURN TO BUFFALO" told of extreme winters that can shut down an interstate. The first Wall Drug billboards appeared outside Buffalo: "Free Ice Water – WALL DRUG." "Homemade Donuts – WALL DRUG."

East of Buffalo, the land started to look like South Dakota, a place I hadn't seen yet, but had imagined. Conical, red anthill peaks, volcanic-looking and covered with grass and sagebrush, dotted the landscape. These gave on to dry tableland and yellow buttes. Some land was carved and sculpted and upward-thrusting, and some rolled in golden, grassy waves to where white clouds sat on the distant lip of the earth.

If only the clouds had been gray. Here, too, people prayed for rain. "We ask dear Lord Jesus Christ to bring rain for our whole region," implored the announcer on KSLT 107.3 FM, who waited for prayer pledges from callers from surrounding communities and acknowledged the prayerful towns that had already called. "Kyle, South Dakota and Hot Springs, South

Dakota have already committed to praying for rain, and we urge more communities to make that commitment."

Sundance, Wyoming wrapped its cowboy tradition around us within an hour of arrival. We sat back on bleachers and watched the whole town turn out to see local seat-of-the-pants toughness in action at the Crook County Fair.

Some of the toughest pants belonged to grammar school kids in full chaps and cowboy hats who tore around barrels and poles so fast I wondered what it must be like to be their mothers, watching their babies streak around the dusty arena at full gallop, cutting edges and corners closer than a buzz cut. We got dirt kicked in our eyes every few minutes, and loved every granule.

Outside the arena fence, pickups and horse trailers sat in the grass, and people led, fed, and groomed their horses. It was kids' rodeo night, with both juniors and seniors competitions, and grade schoolers to teenagers waited outside the fence, controlling varying amounts of nervous energy.

Inside the arena fence, it was take-no-prisoners rodeo.

And, between outside and inside, the rodeo queen reigned from the fence at the chute that fed the riders into the ring. The queen was about 17, and she wore glasses, jet black cowboy hat and jeans, and a cobalt blue shirt of glittering sequins that dazzled and jumped like it was alive. Everyone around was dusty, but the queen sparkled.

I took a picture of her, from behind. She sat on the fence facing left, watching the next rider tuck her nervousness up under her hat and get ready to enter the ring.

Of tens of thousands of photographs shot over 25 years and 50 countries worth of travel, this is one of my favorites. If asked to pick one image that distills the essence of our trip across America after September 11 into a single moment, a moment that evokes the strength and pride and resilience of America's people, and their ability to get back to the business of living and doing what they do, I would choose the picture of the rodeo queen of the Crook County Fair in Sundance, Wyoming.

The rodeo kids were amazing riders. Sharp-turning and lightning fast. Kids with names like Tess and Cody earned blue and purple ribbons, and their parents displayed them on the side mirrors of their pickups or lined them along their dropped truck bed tailgates next to the horse grooming brushes.

"Look at that lil' cowboy!" exclaimed the announcer, as some tiny guy in jeans and boots and hat (how do they stay on at that speed?) raced tight around obstacles and thundered across the arena. Townspeople here know what kind of cowboy a kid is by the time he's 10.

Above us, on the bleachers' top two rungs, sat a group of lean, fit teenagers, all of them, boys and girls alike, with self-assured mountain good looks. "You ride that horse, girl!" They whooped and cheered for their barrel-racing friends the way other high school kids scream for the kids who make touchdowns and slam dunks and speed records in the mile. The harder and faster the riding, the tighter the corners, the louder the hoof-pounding, the dustier the ring, the greater the appreciation and approval from the rider's peers.

Adam preferred the Sundance Motor Inn's cable TV to rodeo, but Dana was utterly enthralled by this magical place where people lived and breathed riding and ranching and rodeo as a matter of course, threads in the fabric of their everyday lives. She saw past the spectacle of the Crook County Fair and realized in a hoofbeat that the people in this town – the kids and teenagers, moms and dads, aunts and uncles, grandmas and grandpas – lived a life centered on land and animals, the outdoors, hard work and hard play. They lived and worked in jeans and cowboy hats. Where we live, people gather for baseball and soccer games. Sundancers gather for rodeo. Dana spoke barely a word while we sat on those bleachers. I could see her thoughts. I could see her eyes take in everything, every detail her senses allowed her to capture. I watched her mind catalogue Sundance, Wyoming as a dream town, the greatest place on earth to live.

Proof positive of the town's magic came when the loudspeaker crackled and the rodeo announcer broadcast the news that there'd be a giant cake to celebrate 4-H's 100th birthday. Everyone was invited to come back to the big exhibition barn where the cake would be cut, "after Karaoke Madness." Surely, heaven must be like Sundance. Horses everywhere and a cake big enough to feed the whole town.

I went out at 6:30 the next morning and ran the neat, tree-lined streets of tiny Sundance and ended up back at the fairgrounds, which sat next to the Crook County Regional School, "Home of the Bulldogs." The yellow school buses that had been parked since June still had last school year's "Who Let The Dogs Out" and "Go Dogs Go" written in white paint all over their windows.

I ran behind the livestock barn where, the night before, we'd taken in the exhibitions and seen prize-winning pigs and cows and champion sheep, wrapped like royalty in little purple coats.

In rose-colored post-dawn, the scene was different. No flash or showmanship, just love, pride and hard work. A dozen or so of the ranchers and farmers who owned these show animals were in the barn, tending to their livestock. Feeding, washing, grooming, patting, talking, whispering. A family gathered around its goat, stroking it. Out back, a lanky teenage boy with long, tousled brown hair nuzzled, soothed and said good morning to his black cow. He held the animal's ears in his hands and rested his chin on the cow's forehead. I left Sundance with this scene of love and deep contentment in my head.

To attract tourists, white men gave an astonishing east Wyoming monolith, with a flat top immense enough to host the mother ship of Spielberg's aliens, the name Devil's Tower. The Sioux call the rock column Bear Lodge.

In Sioux legend, this pillar of land thrust itself from the earth in time to lift seven frightened maidens beyond reach of a hungry bear. The great earth column rose, and carried the maidens to safety. The bear clawed at the monolith as it rose, and the long, vertical claw marks now run from Bear Lodge's flat top to its wooded bottom, and around its entire circumference.

The Sioux also explain the genesis of a piece of night sky through the Bear Lodge legend. The column of land that held the seven frightened maidens rose higher, and kept climbing until the maidens were delivered to the heavens, where they became the constellation Pleiades – the Seven Sisters.

The crowds hadn't yet rolled in when we made our one mile-and-change hike around the base of Devil's Tower through a landscape covered with boulders and rock pillars heaved over eons from the tower's sides to the Ponderosa pine forest below. Six climbers had secured permits to pass beyond the boulder field at the tower's base and try for the summit, and they were part of this singular scene. There was a moment in the sylvan forest that hugged the green, lichen-tinged monolith when I looked on two worlds at once.

Up and to my left, I watched a tiny figure, clad in and hanging from new technology, inch his way up the tower's vertical wall. I looked down and to the right, and saw a tree hung with Native American prayer cloths and prayer bundles filled with offerings of cedar, sweet grasses, and sacred tobacco. On my left, people said, "I'm human. I respect but can conquer you." On my right, people said, "I'm human. I respect and worship you."

South Dakota wasn't far as the crow flies, but it took all day to get there. Just beyond Devil's Tower, in tiny Hulett, where we crossed the Belle Fourche River twice, we met one of the day's several road construction stops. We'd learned many states ago that off-interstate travel means you sometimes have to wait.

We'd sat at construction stops in the Arizona and New Mexico deserts, lined up with scores of cars, vans, RVs, and bikers, waiting for the opposing traffic to travel the single open lane to the end of the line, where we waited. Then, the hard-hatted stop sign holder would turn her sign around, and the Pilot Car would swing in front of the first car in our line and lead us, in single file, to construction's end, where the oncoming queue waited. Once we were safely past, their stop sign holder would signal the all clear, and the Pilot Car would assume position at the front of the new group and lead them back to where we'd come from. Some of these construction zones were 10 miles long, and you sat back, chilled, and got to know the tailgate of the guy in front of you.

At Hulett, population 429, elevation 3,755 feet, our stop sign lady spent our queue's wait talking with two guys in the vehicle just in front of us, a VW Eurovan with Ohio plates. Ignition off, windows down while we waited, I eavesdropped. Hard hat atop her short, straw-blond hair and neon green safety vest over her tank top, she told the VW guys of the tribulations of living in Hulett, so close to Devil's Tower. Hulett was already a Devil's Tower tourism bedroom community. The town - cute, neat as a pin, tree-lined, full of fresh-painted wooden storefronts - was evidently at risk of becoming even more touristy and less Huletty: "They're buyin' up our streets in Hulett! The advertisers. Life's gittin' to be: 'Don't park in front of my house.'"

Of all the construction lines we encountered, which the three of us rather enjoyed because you got to stop and hang with people in a situation none anticipated or initially welcomed but eventually warmed to, Hulett was my favorite.

124

The line consisted of us, the Ohio Eurovan guys, and masses of bikers headed for Sturgis. We and Ohio were the only double-axled vehicles in the group. Two token vans amid scores of gleaming bikes headed for South Dakota, spitting distance away. These bikers had done a little pre-Sturgis sightseeing to Devil's Tower, and now sat in the Hulett construction line with us. I felt like we and Ohio had been adopted by a tribe of chrome-plated, low-riding free spirits. "Okay, New Paint! It's us, Ohio, and a hundred bikes! Enjoy the ride!"

The oncoming traffic line appeared and cleared, the neon stop sign girl turned her sign around, and we followed the Pilot Car across Route 24. The Pilot Car led us to construction's end at Alva, population 50. Everyone was headed to South Dakota, so we continued en caravan to Aladdin, Wyoming, which would feed us to I-90.

I turned the radio up loud. KSKY out of Rapid City was playing a soundtrack ready-made for traveling with Ohio and a nation of bikers heading into South Dakota on a Wyoming mountain back road. We pit stopped en masse in Aladdin, population 15, a number at least quadrupled by the thirsty bikers lining the porch of the Aladdin General Store.

The freedom soundtrack blared from New Paint's radio. John Mellencamp, balladeer of the small town, wailed "Pink Houses," and our heads bobbed as we sang our agreement that America, home of the free, was indeed "somethin' to see."

I played keyboard on the steering wheel, keeping a car length between New Paint's front and Ohio's rear, reveling in the splendor and camaraderie of this high backroads stretch of Wyoming highway. Lynard Skynard was up next, and "Free Bird" never sounded more perfect than it did up on Route 24 that day, western sun lighting up road, forest, mountains and tons of gleaming chrome. Hundreds of wheels spinning, engines purring, clouds gracing the powder blue sky. We travelers were exercising our right to pursue liberty on a beautiful American byway. Our common bond, beyond the construction line we'd fallen into, was that pursuit, and that liberty.

Take that, Osama. You're in a cave, and we're rolling through Wyoming. Plot if you like, but we're moving and doing and smiling at the sound of good rock and roll and the sweet feel of Rocky Mountain breeze lifting our hair and moving coolly over our arms. Boundless beauty, freedom, adventure, possibility. These are ours. We're free birds.

The South Dakota Welcome Center was a cathedral of brochures, staffed by two nice ladies who asked everyone, "How many in your party?" and then requested, with very firm smiles that offered no escape, that you sign the visitor register, which all did, bikers included.

Deadwood's history and great architecture were swallowed by slot machines and kitsch, so I succumbed totally and let the kids hang out at Comfort Inn's Gulches of Fun.

They tried to annihilate each other in the bumper boats. Adam, Dana and one other kid were the only riders, and no one waited in line. The teenager manning the ride was so engrossed in his *Magnum* porn magazine that he let them go at least two rides worth before jerking his head up from the pages and asking them to disembark.

In the bumper car line, a guy from Ohio (not one of our Ohio guys) asked a young South Dakotan about Sturgis and its impact on the area. The boy reported that he and his family vacate their house – go away, stay in a motel, crash with friends or relatives – and rent it to bikers for the week.

"Do they trash the place?"

"Not really."

"What do you get?"

"$5,000. It works."

The Mount Rushmore KOA was too busy for my taste, but the kids had a blast. I let them go off on their own to hang out with other kids, as long as they stayed together and didn't go near water. "Now, get along. No arguing. Adam, be nice to your sister and keep an eye on her. And Dana, do what Adam wants to do, too. Don't be a pain. And if one of you wants to come back to the cabin, you both come back. Nobody goes off alone. Okay?... Okay?..." They were a quarter mile gone. I was talking to myself.

The gargantuan complex, which hosted some massive RVs that stayed for weeks, had 500 sites, two pools, two stores, mini-golf, ice cream shop, arcade, restaurant, pizza parlor, waterslide, basketball court, kids on bikes tearing around the campground's paved roads, horse stable (which Dana volunteered to muck out in the evening, after the hundred or so horses were herded across the road and into the woods to pasture. They bounded out, joyously, free for the night. Their equine body language was completely different the next morning as I watched them return to the stable on my six o'clock run. Heads down, they walked, as slowly as the KOA's wranglers and dog would allow, knowing they were in for a long day of hauling people on their backs.).

Our neighbors were night owls. On one side, a couple from New Jersey pulled in to the cabin next to ours at 2 a.m., and commenced housekeeping setup, using their headlights to illuminate the loud unpacking process. On our other side, a group of Navajo bikers, headed for you-know-where, ate and socialized into the night at their pink plastic-wrapped picnic table. "I want some fry bread, man!"

We were up and out in the morning (after a two-dollar, all-you-can-eat pancake breakfast in the KOA's Big White Tent) before most of the other 499 sites' inhabitants, and we had

Rushmore's giant presidential heads and adjacent giant parking lot almost to ourselves.

*Bury My Heart at Wounded Knee* had, many years ago, changed my view of pieces of our history, history I'd learned in school in the days before honesty became part of the policy.

In my mind, Mount Rushmore was appallingly insensitive, a monument to manifest destiny cut into the sacred hills of people on the receiving end of the dark side of continental expansion, an inescapably huge reminder of white men's domination and theft of the Sioux land it towered above. I respected Gutzon Borglum's artistic accomplishment.    And, I respected the presidents portrayed.

It was the act of chiseling them permanently in that particular landscape that bristled me.   As we drove toward Rushmore, I asked the kids to consider the land around us and try to understand that these hills, this high, curving earth, these stone pinnacles pointing like fingers into the sky, this forest, these deer by the side of the road, were and are revered by the tribes that had called this place home before white men found gold and killed them or pushed them out.  Before the Black Hills became theme parks and fake gold mines and go-kart tracks and wild west shootouts staged for tourists, they were Sioux identity and heritage, and still are. I wanted Dana and Adam to enjoy seeing Mount Rushmore, but I didn't want them looking at it in a naïve and uninformed vacuum.  The rampant kitsch of the Black Hills is dangerous, and I didn't want my kids to be so seduced or anesthetized by it that they gave no thought to the people whose homeland this had been or, indeed, to the beauty and essence of the land itself.

And so, I didn't expect to be moved by Mount Rushmore. To my surprise, I was, feelings intensified by what the country was living through. We all felt it. We stood in the wind at the end of a great walkway lined with flags and plaques of all the states of the union and gazed up at four granite men who'd helped create or preserve or defend America and its ideals at some turbulent or pivotal point in its still-young life. I wondered what they thought as they looked down over us now. Were they gathered in heaven, wanting to help, calling down words of collective wisdom and counsel they hoped we'd hear? Were we listening? If they can be heard above the tumult, calm, experienced voices telling simple truths can be lifelines in times of confusion and pain.

By the time crowds and traffic had begun to thicken around Rushmore, portending a sloth-paced touristic sludge by early afternoon, we were far away, first on spectacular Needles Scenic Byway, then on Iron Mountain Road toward Keystone, catching glimpses of the monumental heads across the valley, the stone portraits framed by the orange and pink spires and rock arches and narrow stone tunnels of these thin, twisting ribbons of high forest road.

Only the strongest of human beings can resist getting off I-90 at exit 110. The land of Wall Drug billboards starts right after Rapid City and holds you in thrall until exit 110, where the giant white water tower carries the name of the town, Wall, on its bulbous tank, and "HOME OF WALL DRUG" on one of the tower's long steel legs. There would be no Wall without Wall Drug, and there would be little to look at along the interstate's dry, yellow monotony without Wall Drug billboards. For the most part, I consider billboards an ugly, even dangerous, distraction. But Wall Drug's are in an interesting league of their own.

They were addictive. You craved the next right after reading the one just gone by. What new message would there be? The billboards were more than marketing, more than advertising genius. They were entertainment and, not unimportantly, stimulants. They kept you alert on that dull, dry, windy stretch of highway. Visual relief from the yellow tedium. Not being alert carried the risk of missing the next message from Wall Drug. When your mind wandered off the road, a new, large rectangle on stilts would appear in the distance just in time, and you'd drive toward it straight and true, eager to see what it said.

Plain lettering on a neutral background devoid of flashy graphics characterized every billboard. Each had a quick message about some road warrior need or interest that the super emporium was prepared to fulfill, and all ended with the words "WALL DRUG" in capital letters: "Free Coffee & Donut for Veterans; Free Coffee & Donut for Honeymooners; Badlands Map; Kids Bored?; Biker Leather at Wall Drug; Garden Burger; Wall Drug Established 1909; Kids LOVE Wall Drug; Travelers Chapel; Western Art; Homemade Lunch Specials; Something to Crow About; We Fit Any Foot; Wood Carvings; Silver Dollar Display; New T-Rex; It's Cool; Homemade Pie; FAST FOOD; South Dakota Original; Rx Museum; Shootin' Gallery; Tour Bus Stop; Wall Drug USA Just Ahead."

The land was yellow rolling prairie and ranchland. Vast, high dryness. Whipping wind. Hay, recently cut, sat in bales, piles of bales, bundles, groups of bundles, blobs, rolls, pyramids of rolls, bricks, stacks of bricks. In the distance I could see a hint of badlands, ridges of pink rock rising along the horizon, veiled by a fog of white desert heat. Farmers and farmers' sons, tan, lean, blue-jeaned, cut more hay, riding John Deeres right up to the kiss of the interstate.

In slow, rich mezzo-soprano, Frederica von Stade sang Copland's vocal arrangement of Shaker Elder Joseph Brackett's "Simple Gifts," and I thought how the gift to be free is, often, far from simple. God may have created it to be so, but men have made the getting and keeping of freedom hard-won and not simple at all.

Half the bikers heading for Sturgis, if they were over 17, let the free South Dakota wind play in their hair as they rode bareheaded, helmets strapped to sissy bars, until the next time they crossed a state line.

Back near Spearfish, just over the border with Wyoming, the Broken Boot Campground had advertised "Showers & Shade." Back there, trees were a hot commodity and a tourist draw. Here, 20 miles from the Badlands, one campground touted "grass" as an amenity. Trees were long since gone. Here, anything green and alive was a draw.

Adam found the street outside Wall Drug as exciting as the roomfuls of merchandise inside. The street was a mass of bikes, Harley and otherwise, parked forks to fenders down the pavement. Adam would have stayed all day to admire each one up close. Had one bike gone down here, the domino line would have stretched out of town, past the water tower, and onto the interstate.

Besides the Wall visit and a spectacular late evening circuit through the nearby Badlands, which glowed like stone on fire in the setting sun, we made three more South Dakota stops, all in a neat line along arrow-straight I-90, before settling into a Kamping Kabin at the Belvedere KOA. (Since New Mexico, we'd come to love these little $35 a night one-room log cozies with bunks and a big bed, a plank desk, mirror, hooks for clothing, electricity, a front yard with a picnic table, a porch with a swing, and a water pump close by. One or both of the kids would yell, "Let's see if there's a KOA!" at the end of many a long day's drive.)

We'd seen billboards - South Dakota's interstate is a petri dish of outdoor advertising, with signs sprouting like vigorous bacteria all along the highway both toward and away from the Black Hills - for Murdo's Pioneer Auto Museum. Car museums had been one of Adam's few requests before we left home, so, by the second billboard, we knew we were headed for Murdo.

We could have spent two days in that museum. A destination unto itself. For old car buffs, this place is worth a plane ticket into Rapid City or Sioux Falls from just about anywhere. We barely scratched the surface of the labyrinthine establishment, resting place for hundreds of the most fantastic antique vehicles on the planet, a warren of barn-like rooms and buildings that held beautiful steel masterpieces. We bought our tickets at the door from the owner.

"Where're ya from?" he asked.

"Boston."

"Oh, you'll wanna see the Metz."

We followed his directions, and found the Metz, an hour later. The directions were flawless, but there was too much antique automotive beauty between us and it to ignore or pass by quickly, and we oohed and awed at everything. Eventually, we came to the exquisite Metz, built in 1908 in Waltham, Massachusetts, 30 miles from our house, and resting now in Murdo, South Dakota. My guess is the owner asks all his visitors where they come from, and, given the remarkable vastness of the collection, I wager he has a "you'll wanna see" car for every one of them.

Our second stop along I-90's unerringly straight South Dakota stretch was in Chamberlain, at a rest area situated high above the wide, winding, muddy-green Missouri River, which we had just crossed at Oacoma. Lewis and Clark had stood here. They'd first met the Yankton Sioux in the hilly landscape that surrounded us. They'd ridden the piece of the Big Muddy we looked upon, although damming had changed the country's longest river into a flow the expedition would scarcely recognize were its members to paddle it today.

Wind played with our hair. Below us, the interstate cut like a knife through the hills. From west to east, a normal sampling of vehicles made its way in the early afternoon sun to Sioux Falls, and perhaps to Minnesota and points beyond. The traffic moving from east to west was a whole different show. A latter day corps of discovery doing 70, clad in chrome, leather, denim, and tattoos. The road was a west-moving blaze of motorcycles, an asphalt river of bikes whose yellow-white headlights shimmered in the heat mirage fog of the stifling South Dakota afternoon. The monster bike rally was ready to roar, and latecomers who hadn't been able to take a week's vacation before the gathering were rolling toward Sturgis in a final hell-bent swell.

An architectural phenomenon is firmly planted in the middle of downtown Mitchell. The Corn Palace is an American artistic statement brilliantly rendered. In corn. Corn art. Art in corn. Corn-as-art. A building made of corn. Covered, embellished, inside and out, with cobs and kernels. A stationary, architectural Rose Bowl Parade in feed instead of flowers. I bought postcards and a corn-shaped candle from a gift shop cashier who told me this year's exterior and interior corn murals "weren't quite done because there hasn't been much rain, and the grain is weak." It looked done to us. Like nothing we'd ever seen. Artists compete annually for the honor of crafting a piece of the next year's Corn Palace. Photographs of Corn Palaces of years gone by lined a lobby wall. The building's skeletal shape stayed the same, but each annual Palace was a new work of iconic American art. Mitchell changes the way you look at corn.

At the Belvedere KOA, where we finally settled in, the high plains wind whipped across the landscape and through the grasses and threw back the curtains of our cabin's open windows. I liked, whenever possible, to leave our cabin or motel room doors open until we went to bed to create a feeling of space to counterbalance the long hours in New Paint. Here, with the door open, we had not only the cabin, the porch and our yard, but the endlessness of the prairie that kept going from there. The view was long. But the wind kept slamming the door shut and blowing pounds of prairie powder through the window and onto our sleeping bags. So, we gave in to nature, closed up, and lived outside until nighttime.

The kids rode little pedal go-karts around the dusty grass between the cabins, made trips to the camp store for microwave popcorn and Chef Boyardee ravioli, and watched a movie in the outdoor "theater," a TV poking through a hole cut in the top of the wall of the shed that held the pool table. The movie was about a dog. It opened to five young viewers, four of whom quickly turned their attention to billiards and video games. Dana remained, sitting alone on a low plank bench in the whipping dust, neck craned upward, head tilted back, until the final credits rolled.

That evening, we sat at our picnic table and tried to keep the frozen pizza we'd bought and microwaved at the camp store from blowing into Minnesota. I'd given up on Sterno, and, as in most campgrounds since New Mexico, the dry conditions in South Dakota warranted campfire bans. But here, even without the parched earth and rainless sky, the wind alone would have made open fire imprudent.

We listened awhile as Almost Willie Nelson, in bandana and braids, sang "You Were Always On My Mind" outside the campground's BBQ cook shack. I thought of the sunset Mike would have seen a few hours earlier and wondered if his had been as beautiful as the plum-colored blaze we beheld. Campers, silhouetted by the night's deep orange- purple sky, listened to the music, swayed, clapped, held hands. A bit of simple pleasure and peace.

While the high prairie night thickened and turned from purple to indigo to black, we sat on our cabin porch around the Coleman lamp, writing, drawing, Gameboying, junk-fooding, talking, listening to wind, and counting stars.

My morning run was a weird and singular treat. First, there was no running with the wind. No matter my direction, it was always headwind. I considered it a two-for-one fitness bonus, like hill running, where I earned both running and resistance training points in a single outing. One deposit, double return. The wind whipped and swirled and sucked up pieces of the campground's dirt road, along which were planted little boards handpainted with observations on life:

"Drive Safely – Not Only Cars Can Be Recalled By Their
Maker"
"Forget the Cake. Go For The Icing"
"Mosquitoes are insects that Make Flies Look Good"
"Life on this earth may be expensive, but includes a free trip
around the sun"
"Vaya Con Dios"

I turned up a narrow yellow farm road that made a straight
cut through an infinite field of chest-high yellow grasses. I felt I'd
disappeared from the world. I was running, in a whirling wind, on
a yellow shaft of dirt, through an endless sea of dancing stalks.
The track went on as far as my eyes could see. But it was remote,
and I was probably trespassing, and I didn't want to mess with a
Plains farmer who might think I was tampering with his irrigation
channels, so I turned around after a mile or so. Before I left it, I
turned for a final gaze down its dun-colored endlessness and
wondered how long and how far it could have carried me.

The wind, the witticisms and the yellow dirt ribbon were
enough to make the run a satisfying sightseeing jaunt, but there
was one more bit of bizarre fun. The farm track emptied onto a
thin paved road where, behind a chain link fence, stood a wall of
cows. Every cow looked at me. Every single bovine stared
directly at me. Dozens of them. Not one chewed, looked
elsewhere, or hung her head in that lazy cow way. Every beefy
face was pressed against the fence, looking at me with giant,
watery eyes. I slowed down and ran in place. I started laughing,
then talking. "Hey, cows! What are all you girls lookin' at?"

Then I noticed a lone cow, hornless head pointed toward me,
up on a rise behind the wall of shuffling, staring moon-eyed
hamburger, and suddenly, she started running down the rise
toward the fence. I froze. Cows don't run! Unless someone's
herding them with dogs or horses or motorcycles or helicopters.
And then, they're not really running, they're being driven. And

they hate it so much there's a word for what they do when they freak out from all that unnatural running: stampede. I had never in my life, anywhere in the world, seen a cow - one who had a choice about it - run. Cows lope, amble, saunter, or sashay, – but they don't run. This cow was building to a full gallop! Of her own volition and propulsion! An unnatural act! What was wrong with this cow? What was she thinking? And what was she going to do? Was she going to try and jump the fence – and her fat sisters – and come after me? I started running, fast, wondering what a cow's best minute-per-mile pace might be. She didn't jump the fence. But I still wonder if I could outrun a cow.

We left Belvedere and headed to Sioux Falls, where we swapped interstates, trading west-east 90 for south-north 29 toward Fargo. The two roads had straightness and wind in common. Wind had buffeted New Paint since the Badlands, and my hands were sore and callused from holding so tight to the wheel. We were headed north to Fargo for two reasons, one practical, one not. I wanted to cross Minnesota at a latitude that would lead to the Great Lakes.

But, I also loved Frances McDormand in the movie. Her beguiling portrayal of pregnant police chief Marge Gunderson put the word "Fargo" on my mind's map. I'd never turned the word over in my head before that movie. It was a dreamy-rough word. Was the place dreamy-rough, too? Did they talk like Frances McDormand's Marge? We had to get through Minnesota on an at least mid-to-northern route to connect to Superior. Launching from Fargo would accomplish that. And, I'd get to hear Fargo.

The travel gods were with me and saw to it that the lights in our $50 motel room didn't come on. I called the front desk and asked for illumination assistance. "Hi. The lights in our room don't work. We have lights in the bathroom, but not in the actual bedroom." Then, on the other end of the line, the first spoken word I heard in Fargo: "Nooo-WAH?" I giggled into the phone and said something along the regrettable lines of, "Wow! I love the way you say 'No!'" The young woman on the other end of the phone used her superb customer service training to make me believe she did not think me a complete idiot.

Within two minutes, she and another young woman knocked on our door. They moved the queen bed back from the wall and plugged in our lights. Surely, I was now the motel's Fool-of-the-Evening, the guest the staff talk about on their breaks or while wishing away the long hours of the night shift. We three needed two young girls to come up, move a bed, and plug a cord in a socket. I imagined the new joke running the Fargo hotel worker circuit: "How many people from Massachusetts does it take to plug a lamp cord into a socket? None! They have North Dakotans do it for them!"

As I stood there in my idiocy, Adam snickering, the lovely front desk clerk who'd solved the light problem said, in a gracious Swedishy lilt, "I doont knoo-WAH, but it might have been the may-UD. When she was vac-YOO-ming. Knocked the ploog froom the wall. Kin we doo anything else fer yoo-WAH?" I started giggling again.

I found an empty socket, plugged in my laptop, and finished my fifth newspaper installment.

The deal was for six stories. I felt a pang of impending loss. One story more, and our transcontinental odyssey would be over. The thought saddened me. The freedom of the road; the freedom of discovery; the joy of being welcomed into people's communities and landscapes; learning their stories; this long, concentrated time with my two precious companions. I didn't want any of it to end. At that moment in Fargo, I transitioned into a new mental and emotional gear. Like a squirrel in fall who eats today's fill and then tucks away the acorns that will carry him through winter, I moved into a mode that let me fully appreciate each moment as it happened, but also let me gather up the trip's past moments, storing them for retrieval, thereby making a place for memory - the beautiful gift which allows a traveler to take the same journey a hundred times.

After I emailed the penultimate installment, we went to El Mariachi Mexican restaurant. We ate superb tacos and burritos, served by a cheery Latina with a big red- lipsticked smile who welcomed us warmly and spoke great Fargo.

## 11

## BIG SEA WATER: Minnesota, Wisconsin

Fargo-Moorhead is really one big place, the Fargo part sitting on the Minnesota border in North Dakota, and the Moorhead part sitting on the North Dakota border in Minnesota. The Red River separates them.

So, because I kept it up for about an hour, I was talking Fargo well into Minnesota, driving the kids, especially Adam, nuts. Payback for "El Camino, Al Pacino," and "Give Dough to the Ethyl Show." Neither Fargo nor Moorhead held much visual appeal that dreary morning, so I thought we could use a little audible entertainment. I was actually imitating a former coworker who hailed from the northern Plains and who turned on the accent whenever he wanted to disarm with folksiness so you wouldn't notice whatever cost-cutting move he was trying to make, usually something involving job elimination. His job was eliminated, don'tcha know.

In Moorhead, a long line of people waited in the dank overcast for the Dakota Boys Ranch Thrift Store to open. The whole scene reminded me of the color gray.

Somewhere near Hawley, Minnesota, "Everything Under the Sun for Good Living," Adopt-a-Highway by the town's Boy Scout

Troop, there was a remarkable change in the topography of the United States of America.

We had left the west. There was no sign, no landmark, but something had clearly happened. Near Hawley, at some spot whose exact position I failed to record, the land turned green.

A palpable current ran through New Paint. Nine and a half thousand miles on the road, and we were riding through green country again. To us, green meant east, and home. It was August. We'd been gone since June. At this point in distance and time away, we were open to a little tug from home, a gentle pull toward familiar ground, a tiny welcoming squeeze. Minnesota's timing was perfect.

I was soon overcome by the realization that the sudden green-equals-east feeling washing over us was, in the truest sense, a watershed. Where the green feeling began and then intensified, blowing the brown and yellow dry-color feelings of the west away from us, scattering them like puffs of dust along Route 10, we were within 50 miles of the place where the Mississippi River is born. The river whose name means "gathering of waters" in Ojibwe, the river that defines the nation's east-west geography, the river that was once the liquid demarcation line between just-born America and lands west, was speaking to us. The green feeling was a message sent by the Father of Waters that we were now within his embrace.

We were pointed due east, and I looked to my right, past Adam, and out the window into the fertile land that rolled away south to the horizon. The water that gathered on the land we drove over today would, three months and 2,300 miles beyond that horizon, reach the Gulf of Mexico. The Louisiana shrimpers we'd driven past in July, docked at Delcambre with their aqua nets furled and hoisted like luminous grasshopper wings, had bobbed in water that had left Minnesota in April. The roiling, brown Mississippi that floated the *Natchez*, whose steam calliope had welcomed us aboard our cruise downriver from New Orleans to

Chalmette had, in spring, been clear, north woods trickles. With this one, long look south out the window, onto and past fields of Minnesota sunflowers, all things were connected.

We didn't need to visit Lake Itasca and wade into the 10-foot-wide headwaters of the Mississippi to feel the great river's power to awe and refresh. Fifty miles from its source, and a hundred miles from any place where the nascent flow had any size to speak of or carried the name Mississippi, we were already renewed by it, and by the profusion of glacial-carved lakes, all sculpted by the retreat of the Ice Age.

Save for the California and Oregon coasts, the absence of water had defined our trip for the 6,400 miles since we'd crossed the Red River at Shreveport, Louisiana the day before entering Texas. Yes, after that we'd crossed the Rio Grande, the Snake, the Salmon, the Missouri and other storied rivers, made friends with smaller beauties like the San Juan and the Truckee, camped at Lakes Powell and Tahoe, gazed into Cascade-ringed Crater Lake's cobalt depths, and driven atop the vast but endangered Ogallala aquifer, intermittently visible wherever Plains irrigation systems sucked out its water and sprayed it over fields of grasses and grains. But, overwhelmingly, the earth had been afire or waiting to ignite, causing people from Texas through the Dakotas to pray for rain and thank God for firefighters. In some places, like the southern reaches of Nevada, there was nothing to burn, and the earth was a parched, brown, treeless void.

I thought of the series of little waterless ironies that will always conjure Nevada for me. I'd picked Rachel, writ big on the map, as an Extraterrestrial Highway oasis, and we dreamt of Dairy Queen cones, but when we reached it, we could see the whole thing in a blink. I mumbled, "That's Rachel. All of it." A slow, sad "All of it..." echoed from the back seats, where the kids were watching *Dennis the Menace*. I sent Adam into the Quik Pik that sat near the Little AleInn, "Earthlings Welcome," to find out about the old mine-like structure in the desert just off the highway. The clerk came out into the blast furnace heat to talk with us, and explained that the old raw mill once took in anything dug from any mine in the area and turned it into saleable commodity. The clerk was a very heavy man in his thirties, and I wanted him to get back to his air conditioning, but we were desert company, and he wanted to talk.

"Where y'all from?"

"Massachusetts."

"Massachusetts! Welllll, thissss…," he said, sweeping his arm over the oven-hot barrenness, "is Nevada." We stood silently for a long moment, looking. Dana, Adam and I saw variations on a brown theme. He saw something more. I looked hard, trying to feel some bit of what he saw in all this dryness. After giving us sufficient time to appreciate the view, knowing the mine structure across the road had brought us into the Quik Pik to begin with, he pointed out another abandoned vestige of Nevada's past he thought would interest us, a derelict silver mine sitting small across the desert on the far horizon.

"What time is it here?" I asked, thinking we might have crossed a time zone since morning. Indeed, our friend confirmed that we'd gained an hour.

"Yer in the Pacific time zone."

"Pacific time zone!" squealed Dana. "That's so weird! There's no water!"

As we pulled away from bone-dry Rachel, passing the "NEXT GAS 110 MILES" sign, which made you check your fuel gauge not once, not twice, but three times, the home-mixed tape I'd been listening to delivered up Smetana's *The Moldau*. As the sweeping symphonic swells evoked the undulating majesty of the great Czech river, we passed carcasses of wild mustangs, brought down by lack of water, lying without eyes in the dust.

Not long after, at Warm Springs, writ medium on the map and with a toponym that promised succor, we'd watched a group of bikers climb a fence at the boarded-up Warm Springs Bar &

Café, ignoring the big red "KEEP OUT" sign. The ramshackle building constituted the entire empty town. The bikers all held canteens, the only containers their bikes had room enough to carry. Empty here meant waterless through the rest of unforgiving Nevada. A few of them stood by a small stream that trickled next to the abandoned café. It looked tempting, but they had likely noticed the cattle in the desert and wisely did not fill up with those waters. They turned their attention to the building itself, hoping to gain entry and find a tap serendipitously still delivering running water. Had there been one or two of them, I would have shared, letting them dip into our cooler, where sloshed this morning's melted ice stocks, New Paint's air conditioning unable to keep that day's ice alive for very long. But a biker's dozen I couldn't help.

Where water had been an elusive, prayed for, and sought after life-giver for so many thousands of miles, now, in northern Minnesota, it flowed in abundance. From this remarkable watershed moment, the presence of water would define the rest of our journey, from here, at the Mississippi's source, to the Hudson, which we'd cross for the second time on our quest, only hours from home, on the trip's last day.

The Minnesota watershed moment was one of the most sudden changes we felt America make as we traveled her. Most of her changes had been slow and subtle, the transition from one climate, topography, economy or culture a smooth, gradual swallow. She eased you into the next part of herself in stages, holding onto pieces of what you were about to leave until you were ready to leave them, quietly slipping in new things, pieces of the places to come. Once you were fully in and of them, and comfortable, the old pieces disappeared. In this marvelous way, America made her vastness accessible and her diversity comprehensible. Somehow, through both her people and the power of the place itself, she was able to be both many and one.

Adopt-a-Highway signs told how dear community is to Minnesotans. Stretches of Routes 10, 34, and 200, the roads that beelined us across the state, had been adopted by groups and organizations, associations and congregations.  Hawley's Boy Scouts had their stretch, and so did the Stablemates 4-H Club, the Lake Park Lutheran Church Youth, the Detroit Lakes AARP, Lutheran Brotherhood Branch 8864, the Wolf Lake Woodchucks 4-H, and scores of small-town churches.

From my rolling vantage point, I formed the impression that citizens of the Lake Country engage in three principle activities: praying, farming and fishing, the relative emphasis and time given over to each, I could not discern.  (Were I to hazard a guess, I'd say, with due respect to the Missouri Synod and the Evangelical Lutheran Church in America, that fishing takes preeminence, preeminence that likely spills over into the other two, with people praying for good fishing and praying for the day's farming to end so they can go fishing.)

Neat Lutheran churches rose in almost every town, and were, indeed, their focal points.  Town hall might be a Quonset hut, as in Lake Park, but the churches were proud, wooden, and crisply painted, with lawns neatly mowed.  There was one in particular, a singular sight, a gorgeous, chocolate-brown clapboard confection trimmed in bright yellow, with a rich brown steeple, sitting on a pronounced rise overlooking a tidy cemetery that met the road. As we passed it, I wrote "Ejsko" in my notes, but I can find no such town name on any map of Minnesota, nor in any atlas or place listing.  Google searching yielded only a suggestion of misspelling. Perhaps it was a high prairie mirage, an illusion, like the Flippin' Ghost of Rough and Ready.

A sign in Detroit Lakes turned a post-9/11 battle cry around: "America Bless God!" and the church in Wildwood reminded folks that "It's Hell Without Jesus."   Graphic and intentionally disturbing anti-abortion signs shouted from otherwise quiet hamlets, and Christian radio played from Moorhead to Duluth.

The water-rich land nurtured deep forests, and yielded corn and grains, beans and sunflowers. Farm stands, tractor dealers, silos, fields under irrigation, turkey farms. Turkey was the local fast food. "Turkey Legs – Eat-In/Take-Out." Towns promoting their annual turkey BBQ's and Harvest Fests. (Signs along the route advertised other must-see events: Music Meltdown, Blues Fest, Faith Fest, and Minnesota's Largest Rodeo, held each July in Park Rapids.)

Man made the churches and carved out the farms, but nature, using glaciers as a tool, made the lakes. Across our route spread a necklace of blue pools, populated with all manner of gilled creatures that lure men into little metal boats where they float for hours, waiting (praying) for a pull.

Height of Land Lake was the first sizeable gem we saw on our trans-Minnesota trek. Then, they began, one after another, forming an endless chain. Sivertson, Twin, Toad, Wolf, Straight, and the biggest at Walker, where Leech Lake never ended. Nevis, population 364, embraced sportsmen with the sign "Welcome Fishermen – 90 Lakes in 10 Mile Radius." Taxidermists sat next to John Deere dealerships. Bait shops rivaled churches for sheer number, and offered golden shiners, leeches, wax worms, redtails, fatheads, crappie, rainbow, suckers, and crawlers. At Park Rapids, 20 miles south of the Mississippi's source, McDonald's parking lot crawled with pickups pulling boat trailers. It was Saturday, and everyone was going fishing after a fast food breakfast. New Paint was one of the few vehicles taking up only one parking space. Most customers required two or three spaces to accommodate their vehicles and trailered boats. The drive-thru line was a scene unto itself. Next to the rigged-out trucks, one packed with six guys in farm caps and sporting the bumper sticker "A MAN AND HIS TRUCK – It's a Beautiful Thing," we looked downright diminutive. Like fish out of water. Non-fishing weenie losers. Not even a decent bumper sticker. We left the fishermen and women to their weekend, leaving Park Rapids on the main road that passed the town funeral home, Cease.

We tooled through places like tiny Akeley, whose giant Paul Bunyan statue made Dana muse, "It'd be funny if you lived here. You could say to your friends, 'Meet me at Paul Bunyan.'" In Walker, self-proclaimed "Fishing Capital of Minnesota," where we were still getting Fargo radio, we hung for awhile at the Walker City Dock on Leech Lake, the biggest lake we'd seen since Tahoe and Crater. I tried to engage the three locals (confirmed by one of their sweatshirts: "Walker, Minnesota Native-Yes, I AM!") standing near Stewart's, which offered Daily Walleye Trips, in conversation, but they weren't keen to talk. Too busy watching the water and the gray wind that was building on it. So, we watched three loons swim around a parked seaplane and drove off, keeping Leech Lake off New Paint's port bow for scores of miles. Leech was an appetizer before the coming feast of truly great lakes.

The day's goal was Duluth. Gritty, tough and worn, but beautiful in the way of honest, hard-working places. Like a Sandburg poem. I love such places, cities of big shoulders that merit respect because of what they were or made or shipped or grew or mined in their primes, and what they are now, either holding on, reinvented, or trying to do either or both.

The renovated Canal Park Waterfront was hip and gentrified, but the real Duluth spilled in a brick and clapboard jumble down the high, broad lakefront hill that ends at Superior's shore. We went down by the ship berths, many empty, and by the grain elevators and lakeside docks piled with grain and coal, and watched the late afternoon sun paint Duluth's mountain of old brick and painted wood with a palette of Rust Belt colors. It wasn't Sandburg's Chicago, but as it spread and climbed and sparkled and splashed in elegant toughness, it seemed to me "set vivid against the little soft cities."

I'd planned to overnight in Duluth. We were all well beyond the point of needing to get out of the van and nest somewhere. We'd driven over 300 miles already that day from Fargo to Duluth, and the day before had been the trip's record-setter, with 469 miles logged between Belvedere and Fargo. Even though they'd rolled over nearly 800 miles in the last two days, my incredible companions whined not a whit. I didn't expect them to, knowing as they do that some travel days are work days. They've been through the "today's not gonna be an easy one" drill all over the world. Some days, you have to start moving when you'd rather stay put, and keep moving when you'd rather stop. I knew they were beat, but they kept it to themselves.

I grew increasingly apprehensive the longer lodging eluded us because in the morning I had to start marathon training. I'd be running according to a strict schedule from tomorrow on. Day one would be an early eight-miler, the longest I'd run in nine months. And, I'd have to be out at dawn to complete the run and still hit the road at a respectably early hour. I didn't want the first day of training to be unpleasant, and I needed liquids, carbs and sleep, or I'd be in for at least a bit of misery. I needed a hotel and a restaurant. We all did.

Minnesota may have 10,000 lakes, but it has no vacant hotel rooms on the Lake Superior shore on a summer weekend. Duluth was booked solid. Hotel desk clerks shook their heads at me as soon as I walked through the door. "Nothing." Not at any price. I pushed north from Duluth on old Route 61, a scenic byway that hugs Superior's shore – a road I'd hoped to explore at a less urgent pace - thinking we'd find something along this popular vacation stretch. The drive is spectacular, but the beauty was pretty well lost on us as we passed one "NO VACANCY" sign after another. The hours were slipping by, and I began to fret. Not a bed or campsite to be had. No berth available at North Shore Cottages, The Inn on Gitchee Gumee, Lake Breeze Motel, Gardenwood Motel & Cabins, Heinzs' Beachway, Spinnaker Inn, Dodges Log Lodges or Emily's Eatery & Inn.

At Two Harbors, the Country Inn desk clerk made a valiant round of phone calls, trying to find us somewhere to bunk. (I offered her a hundred bucks to sleep in her garage. She laughed and said, "Oh, that's an idea. When my teenager moves out, maybe I'll rent it.") Her phone calls confirmed there were no vacancies anywhere, all the way up to Silver Bay. She did uncover an inn that had one room left, but the owner wouldn't rent it to me because of "the child." Dana was "the child." I took the phone and explained that Dana wasn't really a child, but a traveler who'd spent the last six weeks traversing 9,700 miles of America, and who, I could guarantee, would not deface the inn's bedroom or disturb other guests. No dice. Chronological was the only age the innkeeper cared about.

Since we were driving farther out of our way and in the wrong direction, I gave up at Two Harbors, drove back down to Duluth, and crossed the steel John Blatnik Bridge to Superior, Wisconsin. Superior sits just across from Duluth, but it's not a mirror image. Superior evoked no Sandburgesque "proud to be alive and coarse and strong and cunning." Just grim and ugly.

Made memorably uglier by the desk clerk at a big chain hotel (and by the hotel itself which, had it put out a "No Vacancy" sign, would have saved dozens of travelers from an unpleasant face to snout encounter with Ms. Superior.)

This porcine young woman stands out not only for her rudeness that night as road travelers supplicated at her (cold) reception desk and were told, with grinning, evil relish, directed at each pilgrim personally and individually, " We're full. We're totally filled," but she also stands out because she is one of only two deeply unpleasant people we encountered on our entire transcontinental journey.

(I consciously eliminate the Panaca, Nevada gas station crew from consideration, forgiving them on the assumption that they'd been out in the sun too long. And, to cut the state of Nevada a break, I decided to cancel them out with the only other human beings we spoke with during our southern Nevada traverse, both lovely - the Rachel Quik Pik clerk and the nice lady who sold us ice cream bars in Tonopah, "Home of the Muckers." She pointed out the 1906 Mizpah Hotel and the derelict silver mine hulking above the town, and made sure we didn't leave her store without learning some of the town's old silver history and knowing that Miller's Rest Area just down the road had a public pump offering "Fresh Water.")

That Ms. Superior stands out in her rudeness says much about her (and the other prize-winner, the ranger we bought our Mesa Verde tour tickets from, described in Dana's journal as, "the jerkiest ranger in the world"). But, it says more about the rest, about Americans from one corner of the country to the other. We'd observe, meet or spend time with hundreds of people in 24 states before the end of our travels, and for only two of them to be actively nasty is a tribute to everybody else. There's more power in a gentle nod than a superior smirk.

The times America found herself in no doubt contributed to our collective civility toward and respect for one another. We were healing together from the largest wound we'd ever suffered, and, by simply being kind, we gave and took comfort and reassurance. But, on this long and beautiful journey, we learned how deep our country's goodness ran, goodness that September 11 didn't create. It's been there. It's still there. September 11 only opened the well wide and made sure the pumps were working. As we left the completely full hotel that employed Ms. Superior, I thought it wonderful that she was such an outlier. We broke open the Ritz Bits and pushed on.

We made our acquaintance with Route 13, which would, after an inland spell through remote, rural farmland, become a lake-hugging ribbon of wild beauty.

At tiny Cornucopia, smack on whipping, wind-tossed Superior, we found a room at Rich and Glenda Zbien's tiny South Shore Motel, the sweetest place we'd ever seen. We rang the buzzer in the motel office and watched Mrs. Zbien walk across the lawn from the big white house behind the motel and enter the office through a back door. She took our $54 and checked us in with few words. When I parked New Paint for the night, I logged the day's final odometer reading. In the past two days, we'd driven 850 miles, from Belvedere, South Dakota to Fargo, North Dakota, to Cornucopia, Wisconsin. I shared the statistic with the kids. Adam shook his head. "I can't believe we woke up this morning in North Dakota." Just uttering the sentence seemed to exhaust him. Indeed, Fargo seemed a lifetime away.

From our motel room window, we watched whitecaps crash across Lake Superior, which lapped at the shore just across the road, a stretch of which had been adopted by the South Shore Parrot Heads. Adam liked it here, because the Zbiens had a purple Mustang parked in their yard.

I woke before dawn, ready to run. A "NO VACANCY" sign had appeared during the night. Seagulls screamed. I punched 72 minutes into my chronograph, and headed out for eight miles. My pace ranges from 7.5 to 10-minute miles, depending on distance, weather, mindset, sleep, body fuel, phases of the moon, planetary alignment, who's President, and any number of other factors, so using nine-minute miles ensures, and usually beats, the required mileage.

I ran around the small marina and public harbor and scattered the scores of seagulls sunning on Cornucopia's red sand beach. They screeched and whirled and headed out over Superior's wind-whipped surface. I ran the hills fore and aft the quarter-block that Cornucopia calls downtown. Past Fish Lipps, where we'd dined the night before. Past Ehlers Store, which stocks just enough to enable Cornucopians to delay shopping trips into Superior. Past the "Northernmost Post Office in Wisconsin." The hills were a glorious piece of cake, and I thanked God for all those preparatory runs at altitude from Tahoe to the Black Hills. They weren't much for mileage, but they'd built me up, and I took the comfortable Cornucopia run as a good omen that my 10 weeks of training would go well. Dana shot up from her sheets when I unlocked the motel room door.

"How was it?"

"It was good, Dane. Really good."

"Good. I'm glad." And she hunkered back under the covers for a few more minutes of sleep while I showered and packed up New Paint. I rousted the troops for the next stage of our adventure, and they nestled in the van with their blankets and pillows, and ate Pop-Tarts and fruit cocktail while we drove deeper into the land of the Big Sea Water.

We would have a Great Lake beside us for most of every travel day from Cornucopia, Wisconsin to Erie, Pennsylvania. We rolled at an easy pace through or alongside Chippewa reservations; fish hatcheries; trout smokehouses; coves and inlets where wild rice, harvested by the Chippewa, grew close to shore; lakeside beach communities; fishing camps; once-bustling iron ore cities; federally-protected islands and lakeshores; powder-white beaches; red sand beaches; red dirt tracks shooting off paved roads; fields studded with hay rolls; brown rivers that emptied into the sea-like lakes; dense and primal forests. Most places were gritty, funky, a little edgy, the people unpretentious regular folk who gave you short, honest answers.

Superior's wild, pine-ringed beaches, often 50 feet from our van, were magnets. We couldn't drive by one without stopping, and we developed a Superior beach routine. We'd pull off, and I would do housekeeping tasks like trash bucket emptying, rearrangement of drying laundry, journal writing. Dana would run and whoop along the sand and chase seagulls, and Adam would build sculptures from twigs, branches, rocks, feathers and charred firewood that he found along the beach. He'd leave a string of these enigmatic creations along Great Lakes shores from Cornucopia to Port Clinton, Ohio.

"People will come to this beach and wonder what this piece of art is, what it's all about," I said, as I looked on his first sculpture.

"Okay."

"They'll think there's some message here, something to do with the land, the lake, the native people who live here." I fished for hints of what Adam thought about as he built this art.

"Okay."

"This is cool. People will wonder who made this, what it means, and whether it's some symbol honoring the beauty of this place."

"Okay."


Bayfield, Wisconsin (No Vacancy) is one of those places whose gingerbread perfection, almost too much to believe, makes you want to stop and stay for longer than your allotted time, be that an hour, a day, a summer vacation, or a lifetime. A privileged place, with sweeping views and Victorian painted ladies, an elegant gem built on a sun-drenched hillside overlooking Gitchee Gumee and the Apostle Islands National Lakeshore, exquisite yachts and private sailing vessels at anchor in North Harbor.

While Bayfielders gathered for the 10 a.m. service at Bayfield Presbyterian Church, announced by a lilting carillon that rang up and down the hilly streets and through the old town of brick and wood and sandstone and cobbles on and around Rittenhouse Avenue, we took the ferry to lush, pine-forested Madeline, an Apostle not administered by the National Park Service. We drove off the ferry at LaPointe (No Vacancy) and explored the island's red sand beaches and fern-carpeted woods.

Getting Dana on the boat took a little doing. I'd been singing "The Wreck of the Edmund Fitzgerald" since South Dakota, and the kids had found the doomed freighter's name and picture on the Shipwreck Map that had hung near the bar at Fish Lipps back in Cornucopia. That there were so many other Gitchee Gumee victims on the map stunned a bit and made you look over this white-capped water with respect and awe. Together, the Great Lakes have claimed over 6,000 ships.

"What if it's like the boat ride in Polperro? What if she rolls?" moaned Dana, bringing us all back to a rough little ride off the Cornwall coast some years back. The wooden boat, an open dory that sat a dozen passengers aft, had bucked and pitched in the growing seas that met her gunwales, and I remember noting with great alarm the absence of life jackets. I'd just positioned every one of us on a presumably floatable seat cushion, when the skipper made a joke, one that made most of the passengers' already terrified faces go sheet white. "If she rolls," he boomed, "just swim underneath 'er and come up on the other side." To this day, "If she rolls…" denotes any situation with the potential to induce terror.

Before getting on the Bayfield to Madeline ferry, we'd had a little talk with the ranger at the Apostle Islands Visitor Center up the hill in town, where we'd stopped to see the working Fresnel lens that once topped Michigan Island Light. I'd explained our hesitancy toward going out on the lake that sent the *Edmund Fitzgerald* to the bottom. The ranger looked directly at Dana and assured her, "It should be no problem out there today," the caveat that nature makes the rules, built lexicographically into her reply by the word "should," appreciated only by me. (Perhaps. I could be underestimating my children.)

The *Edmund Fitzgerald* went down in 1975, all hands lost. Some of the 29 crew members hailed from cities and towns we'd come to know during our days along the Great Lakes. The ore freighter put out from Superior, Wisconsin, bound for Detroit, then Cleveland. I'd seen the word "TACONITE" emblazoned on a massive Burlington Northern Santa Fe facility we'd passed in Superior, and wondered if the *Edmund Fitzgerald's* load had come from there. Mined taconite was and is the stuff that iron ore and, eventually, steel, comes from. The hard rock contains iron, which is extracted, turned into pellets, and, in the days before American steel started its decline in the face of cheaper foreign product, was loaded into the endless queues of freighters that plied the waters and took the raw cargo to once bustling Great Lakes' steel mills. Ore is still mined, ships and railcars are still loaded, steel mills still spit out product, but cheaper overseas steel has stolen much of the Rust Belt's energy and output.

The *Edmund Fitzgerald* had been part of the chain of rugged tasks that took rock dug from mines and turned it, ultimately, into the factories, ships, railroads, skyscrapers, tanks, planes and automobiles that built, bolstered and defended America. The *Fitz* ore was bound for Detroit, where it was to have been made into cars. She took on her cargo at the city, Superior. That cargo, 26,116 tons of taconite pellets, surrounds her now, 530 feet under the lake, Superior.

Of the 29 *Fitzgerald* men who died on November 10, 1975, 12 were from places we'd touch and that would touch us on this journey. We would pass through these men's hometowns:

Fred Beetcher, 56, Porter, Superior, Wisconsin
Thomas Borgeson, 41, Maintenance Man, Duluth, Minnesota
Ransom Cundy, 53, Watchman, Superior, Wisconsin
Allen Kalmon, 43, Second Cook, Washburn, Wisconsin
Joseph Mazes, 59, Special Maintenance Man, Ashland,
Wisconsin
Ernest McSorley, 63, Captain, Toledo, Ohio
Eugene O'Brien, 50, Wheelsman, Toledo, Ohio
Karl Peckol, 20, Watchman, Ashtabula, Ohio
Robert Rafferty, 62, Steward, Toledo, Ohio
Paul Rippa, 22, Deckhand, Ashtabula, Ohio
John Simmons, 63, Wheelsman, Ashland, Wisconsin
William Spengler, 59, Watchman, Toledo, Ohio

That places like Duluth, Washburn, Ashland and Toledo, rugged red sandstone places, produced fathers and sons who lived, worked, and sometimes died on Great Lakes freighters fit. Tough, hard-working places create tough, hard-working men. Or maybe it works the other way round.

As we moved through America we were, for periods of time that were always too short, part of so many places that radiated pride, history, industry, honesty, these strengths sometimes lying beneath a tired, wizened surface, making you scratch a bit to find whatever gave the place its meaning.

As we approached Ashland, Wisconsin on Route 13, something singular appeared. The road rode high, and the view opened into a wide sweep. Something monstrous and hauntingly gorgeous jutted a quarter-way out into Chequamegon Bay. It was clear it was a ruin, once powerful and important, now disused. It looked like a bridge, an aqueduct, a railroad trestle, a giant pier. It was mysteriously beautiful.

Ashland's Soo Line oredock was the first of several we'd see on the Great Lakes, mammoth, hulking vestiges of the once mighty iron and steel industries. Colossal steel and wood cathedrals across whose tops ore-laden railroad cars had rolled to the literal end of the line and dumped their cargo into the holds of freighters waiting in the water below, freighters like the *Edmund Fitzgerald.*

Ashland seemed a Carl Sandburg place. He would have found poems here, I think. A crimson sandstone city that once pulsed to the beat and brawn of arriving and departing ore trains and ships. The rich red stone and towering silvery-white steeple of Our Lady of the Lake Catholic Church commanded the hillside above the bay and glowed in the intense sun as if afire. Vivid murals with scenes from Ashland's history adorned the old brick sides of buildings all over town. Main Street was a parade of exquisite late 19th century red sandstone buildings and big old banks like Greek temples, built, I imagined, to hold all the iron, railroad and freighter money of an earlier Ashland. Main Street rivaled the best of the scores of pridefully preserved old American downtowns we rolled through on this journey, downtowns that wore their pasts like medals and badges of honor, and that presented a looking glass into our history, history sadly overlooked or, worse, lost, in the numbing sterility of strip malls and interstates.

The longer we spent in it, the more I loved Ashland.

But it was the great black and rust oredock that kept drawing us back. A mammoth ribcage, gritty and haunting. It captivated, then choked you with melancholy. I couldn't leave it.

The $20-a-night RV sites next to Kreher Park sat in the shadow of the leviathan oredock whose last load shipped out in 1965. The campers could boat, swim, read in a chair on the beach, or consider the mighty rusting ore chutes overhead that ran the length of the massive dock. We parked under the rail approach to the dock, and looked up between the wooden ties and steel rails and imagined the great Soo Line cars rolling over our heads out over the water to the end of the dock, freighters lined up, hungry holds open and agape, metal clanging, ore pellets booming down endless chutes called pockets, men yelling, whistles wailing.

Up the road at Bayview Park, some kids dashed down a wooden swimming pier, screeching and hollering as they jumped off into cold Superior. Their parents sat at a picnic table under a tree and ate chips and big sandwiches. The kids would jump off, swim to the beach, catch their breath, then whoop again down the pier. The parents were consumed by their food, so the lean, young lifeguard was left to monitor every pier-length dash, every leap off the edge, and every swim back to shore, making sure every kid was at all times accounted for. He shared bits of oredock info between leaps and dashes.

"We're the Oredockers," he said, of Ashland's high school sports teams. (I imagined him the star quarterback.) He pointed to long, straight rows of seagulls sitting in the water near the pier we stood on. "That's an old dock right there." We looked closer, and saw the submerged remnants of an oredock, now just flooded pilings that made excellent bird pedestals. The exact skeleton of the dock was revealed by visually connecting-the-gulls. "There used to be seven or eight oredocks right here around Ashland," said the blond Speedoed teenager before he sped off again to check on the running, leaping, swimming triathletes.

## 12

## MORE SHORES: Michigan, Ohio

Route 13 turned into Route 2 as it made for the Michigan border at Ironwood, whose old theatre had a perfect vintage marquee. Ironwood, whose first ore mine shaft was sunk in 1885, is also home to Hiawatha, "The World's Tallest Indian," 52 feet and 18,000 pounds of fiberglass, crafted by Gordon Displays of Minneapolis. We didn't treat Hiawatha the way the Chamber of Commerce likely intended. Instead, at whose suggestion I can't remember or won't admit, our trio degenerated completely and stood between Hiawatha's mongo moccasins and looked up under his fiberglass buckskin "at his butt," an immature act that had us giggling for miles.

Route 28 took us across the top of the Upper Peninsula, and we drove through a chain of north woods backcountry towns, each with its own version of the basics: gas, store, church, bait shop, fire station, post office, café, and maybe a small motel. This was fishing and hunting heaven, and, in winter, snowmobile and ski country. Gogebic County was now a sportsman's paradise, but the Gogebic Range was full of iron, and it was Gogebic ore that had fed Ashland's once hungry dock.

At Bergland, established 1902 and "Home of the Vikings," we read a sweet sign: "Entering Eastern Time Zone." The kids cheered. I felt a rush of homesickness. As we drove through the immaculate little town, we called Mike to tell him all four of us were once again spinning around on planet earth in the same time zone.

As the woodsy, rural inland towns began to blend together into a straight, monotonous chain – Ewen, Bruce Crossing, Sidnaw, Champion (which distinguished itself as the "Horse-Pulling Capital of the U.P."), Humboldt, where we passed a billboard for Da Yoopers Tourist Trap (miles and miles elapsing until I equated Yoopers with U.P.'ers), we came to Marquette, one of the most beautiful small American cities I have ever seen.

For 9,900 miles, I'd been keeping a list in my head. A list of communities I held as special. These towns had, for different reasons and in different ways, especially touched me. When I thought of them, I smiled from the inside out, and that's what they had in common. New River Gorge, Lexington, Memphis, Natchez, New Orleans, Santa Rosa, Acoma, Santa Fe, Bluff, Lee Vining, Fort Bragg, Bend, Boise, Red Lodge, Sundance, Belvedere, Duluth, Ashland.

I added Marquette, Michigan to the list. She sat on hills above Superior, her old neighborhoods collections of trim, fresh-painted, wooden workingman houses set amongst mature trees, streets undulating up or down depending on one's orientation to the lakeshore. Her downtown was a wonder of fire-red stone and brick.

If Ashland had been beautiful red sandstone, Marquette was beautiful red sandstone on steroids. Marquette's historic districts brimmed with Classical Revival, late Victorian, Gothic, Italianate and Romanesque buildings, and these last called loudest.

I live in a town whose past and current beauty owe almost everything to one family whose fortune from shovel manufacture allowed the commission of works, all within blocks of my home, from such artisans of their day as Frederick Law Olmsted, John LaFarge, Fletcher Steele, Augustus Saint-Gaudens, Stanford White and Henry Hobson Richardson. It was Richardson's magnificent Oakes Ames Memorial Hall, an architectural poem in glowing red stone that sits around the corner from my house, which made me want the house to begin with. The house needed work when we found it, but if Richardson had rolled up his sleeves in this neighborhood, how could we walk away? And so, I loved Marquette on sight because I was primed to. I'd lived 13 years daily drinking in the beauty of H.H. Richardson's sandstone.

I could make another possible connection between my town's streets and Marquette's. A link forged by old steel rails. The Ames shovels, fortune, and family that brought Richardson to my town played key roles in the building of the transcontinental railroad. When rail became king, Richardson would design ornate railroad stations, one of which sits two blocks from my house. In the late 19th century, as rail moved the goods and grains and ores of the nation, stations from Detroit to Chicago were built in Richardson's Romanesque style. And, great Richardson-inspired buildings of colossal sandstone appeared in the downtowns and civic hearts of railhead cities in the Upper Midwest. Perhaps the builders of Marquette's imposing, beautiful downtown had looked on photographs and plans of the buildings that grace my little village before they erected their own crimson halls and churches.

I'd fallen under the spell of Marquette's architecture and undulations and hilltop setting above the bay. By the time we laid eyes on the oredock, Marquette had already shown enough treasures to make it hard to leave. We checked into the Super 8, $45, with indoor pool, Jacuzzi, free breakfast, and a view of Superior at the end of the long Route 41 downhill run to the lakefront. We'd play, swim, eat and rest, and give the oredock our full attention in the morning.


I figured God put him there on purpose. We'd driven down to Matson Park at Lower Harbor, eye level with the oredock. The kids ran around and did kid things while I eavesdropped on two old men discussing pike. Seagulls buzzed my head while I shot pictures. I turned around to check on the kids, and there he sat.

A twenty-something guy with spiked yellow hair and blue-tinted sunglasses sat inside the trunk of his car listening to music pulsing from speakers that should have been on a living room floor. He stared out at the oredock. He had to have been purposely sent for me to talk to, because it was too early for someone that age, unless he had to get up for work (it was Monday, so a possibility, although he didn't seem to be going anywhere) to be out of bed.

I approached the trunk and introduced myself. He turned down his music and began telling me about the oredock, which he clearly loved. He spoke with passionate intelligence.

He was from Ishpeming, a gray place we'd passed through. He sat in the trunk and told me how everything had once worked. He described an ore loading, from the train's approach, to its screeching crawl out over the water to the end of the dock, to its dumpers opening wide, to the pellets screaming down the pockets into the ship's hold, to the freighter sitting lower and lower as its load mounted.

And then he turned to today. "The Marquette dock closed down about 10 years ago, maybe more. The only working dock in the area is at Presque Isle."

"Is the Presque Isle dock busy?"

"Yeah, pretty busy. The Chamber of Commerce should have a ship schedule, but if you spend the better part of a day there, you should see a ship."

Presque Isle was north, and we had to head south, so I asked him to tell me more, to paint more pictures of what it was and is like to live here.

"Cheap foreign steel is flooding the economy, and it's a real pain in the butt." He said there were only two operating ore mines in the area, Tilden and Empire, both run by the giant Cleveland-Cliffs corporation. "Ishpeming's mine is closed down. They're thinkin' of makin' it into an amusement park."

There were more old ore mines around than working ones.

"Ya know Negaunee?" he asked, looking at me through his blue lenses.

"Yes. We drove through it. Pretty lake. Had a gorgeous brown stone church with mint green and white trim. My daughter said it looked like a cake. Like a gingerbread house."

"Yeah. Well, there's an old mine there, on school premises. Negaunee High School's built over an old mine shaft. You can still go down in it."

"What about Marquette's oredock? What's happening with that?"

"They're deciding whether to tear it down. Public safety. For now, they show fireworks over it on the 4$^{th}$ of July."

I thanked my friend for his time. He shook my hand, said to have a good trip, and turned his music back up.

On our way out of the city, we passed the Vierling Brewery & Restaurant's rear brick wall, the wall that faces the harbor, the oredock, and the old end of the rail line. Huge letters painted on the wall said, "UNIONS – The People Who Brought You The Weekend."

On Front Street, near Getz' Clothing Store and close to Superior and the Marquette dock, we looked up at chunks of train trestle flanking each side of the street. No track ran between them, just deep blue sky. With the removal of the old train approach, the piecemeal disassembly of Marquette's oredock had begun long ago.


Route 28 to Munising offered sweeping Superior views, and the Big Sea Water indeed looked like an ocean, limitless, deep steel blue, alive with waves and whitecaps. I kept marveling that we'd been driving along this same water for three days, and what we'd seen was only a small part of its southern shore. When I put it that way, the kids would take a long look, trying to get a mental grasp around a lake so big that just this little piece of it could stay outside the car window for three days. As we considered all this water, National Public Radio news announced that Mesa Verde had been closed. A fire ignited by a lightning strike had destroyed employee and ranger homes, but none of the cliff houses had been damaged. We thought of slump-suffering Honest Ranger. We thought of Spruce Tree House. We thought of the charred skeleton trees and the kiva endurance contest. Perhaps Adam thought of Amanda from California. The National Park Service hoped to reopen to tourists within a week.

At Shelter and Au Train Bays, where wide arcs of beach were ringed by towering pines and massaged by the ebb and flow of Superior's waves, I wrote, Dana galloped like a wild horse along the sand, and Adam crafted mysterious rock and log sculptures.

The A&W Root Beer stands I'm familiar with sell hot dogs. The sign at Munising, Michigan's A&W said, "Try Our Whitefish Sandwich." Of course. What else would a fast food joint in the Hiawatha National Forest serve? Besides fish, the ubiquitous U.P. food was pasties, the original pocket sandwich born of the need to take something substantial and easy to handle underground into mines. Adam, a meat-eater, was our resident pasty expert, having sampled his first years ago in Cornwall, the beef and onion-stuffed half-moon of crust about as big as he was then. I remember the smile he'd wore while he ate it. Here, in the Upper Peninsula, pasties, more for tourists than miners, were everywhere. "Grama's," "Muldoon's," "Award-winning." "Fishing Tackle & Hot Pasties." "Homemade." Pasties from one end of the U.P. to the other.

My plan had been to take a boat from Munising ("Snowmobile Capital of the World") along Pictured Rocks National Lakeshore. But, because of the "if she rolls factor," we ended up driving the lakeshore, seeing only Miner's Castle, one of scores of rock formations, all best seen from the water. Unless the water is rough.

I'd stood in the boat cruise ticket line and heard the ticket seller tell people ahead of me "the seas are rough." They bought tickets. Perhaps they'd never had a Polperro dory experience, but we had, and I was going to ask some questions.

"I heard you say the seas are rough. How rough?"

"Oh, it is churning up a bit."

"How high?"

"It's getting a little high."

"How high? I really need to know. Because of the kids."

"It's about three to four-foot waves."

"Are the boats getting tossed around?"

"They've got stabilizers to prevent side to side rocking, but there's still lots of front to back."

I polled the family. Dana wasn't going. Neither was I. Adam looked at it like a theme park ride and couldn't wait to board, but he wasn't going alone.

"Thanks. I think we'll see what we can see from the car."

I was fascinated by the scene of people lined up to buy boat tickets to go out onto Lake Superior, a known killer, which was whipping itself into an ever mightier froth with each passing minute. Groups of white-haired seniors, some with canes; families in sandals and sunglasses and sports team t-shirts; young couples holding hands. I stood beside an unmanned radio near an unused souvenir counter, and overheard captains who were out on the water talking about how rough it was, and how it was getting worse. "I'm gonna show 'em the Castle, then take 'er in." Two minutes later, the cruise line canceled all departures and the ticket holders queued up again, this time for refunds.

We turned inland and said goodbye to Superior. Straight, forested Route 94 cut across the U.P. to Manistique, where we got our first glimpse of Lake Michigan just after passing the Redi-Mix Concrete Company, whose product, burial vaults, lay stacked in the yard right next to the road, some vaults tipped on end, cement covers off, so you could contemplate the interior room of a Redi-Mix sarcophagus.


"LAKE MICHIGAN." I wrote it in capital letters in my journal.

I knew Lake Michigan. I'd first met it as a kid when we'd lived in Libertyville, Illinois, a Chicago suburb. We'd go into the city to the Field Museum and the Adler Planetarium, whose lakefront settings were as exciting to me as anything inside. I remember the words "Lake Shore Drive" and "the Loop" bandied about the house as my dad talked about his work day on his salesman's beat, restocking stores in his downtown Chicago territory with Rust Craft greeting cards and wrapping paper.

When, years and many moves later, I got my own beat, selling insurance and training other people to sell it, Chicago was one of the places I traveled to. On every business trip, I'd steal a few hours, head north, and drive to Fairlawn Avenue in Libertyville. On my last trip, the owners of the house we'd lived in were in the front yard. I parked across the street and walked over to the house, the one my parents loved more than any other house they've owned.

"Hi. I'm Lori Hein. Sorry to bother you. I used to live here, some 30 years ago."

"Oh! Your father must be the one who built the sunburst patio!"

In an instant, I was invited inside. We walked through the garage, and I heard echoes of the summer day camp I'd run there with my friend, Judy. I was 11. Judy was 12. We hosted neighborhood kids, did arts and crafts, played games, served snacks, got our pictures in the town paper. We charged ten cents a kid. The kids' mothers got four hours of free time for a dime. My mother got four hours of making sure everyone else's kid was safe while in the care of her own, bigger kid. Judy and I split the money down the middle, thinking it was profit. My mother bought the Kool-Aid and lemon wafers we served as snacks.

I stepped onto the round, red, sunburst patio from the back room off the garage. My dad built this. I'd watched him dig the dirt circle out of the earth. Roll the red and yellow bricks he'd scouted from contractors and construction sites in his wheelbarrow and pile them on the back lawn. Lay them, with an artist's eye, into a brick sun with a yellow middle that we could sit on, a brick sun that no one else in Butterfield Estates, our development that had been cut out of a cornfield, had.

I thanked the family. I don't remember their name. I told them I'd tell my dad people were still enjoying his sunburst patio after all these years. The whole family lined up outside 1044 Fairlawn Avenue and waved as I drove away in my rental car.

So, perhaps because Lake Michigan figured as a peripheral part of one of the many homes I've had in my life, reaching it was like reaching a small piece of home. This great lake was part of me, was a known, and I felt our journey enter the realm of things familiar. The feeling was bittersweet.

We stood on Manistique's public beach, just up the road from the tomb-filled Redi-Mix lot. Something else about Lake Michigan stirred feelings that went beyond simple contemplation of a great and storied hard-working American lake. I pointed at the horizon.

I told the kids, "If you kept going straight down the lake from where we're standing, from this very spot, you'd come to Chicago. It's sitting right on the lake at the other end. It's facing us. We're standing on Michigan's northern shore, so let's say we're 'up.' Chicago sits on the south shore, straight down from where we are right now."

"Okay," said Adam, taking a break from construction of a sculptural enigma of stones, shells and driftwood. He turned toward the water, considering it and the great unseen city at its other end, a city he'd heard me talk of from time to time. He knew Chicago had some connection to my life.

"It's 300 miles away, but it's sitting right down there." We stood and looked out over the vast blue expanse, like Superior, sea-like and immense beyond comprehension. Chicago, reinvented from its days as hog butcher to the nation, sat gleaming, as the gull flies, "right down there." Right down there, just beyond what the earth's curvature allowed our eyes to see, stood the elegant structures of Sullivan and Wright and the cloud-piercing glass and steel towers America has erected as their successors.

The thought of Chicago at the end of this water both excited and unsettled me, and I sat on Manistique's powdery white beach to think about why.

With some exceptions, I had purposely avoided big cities on this trip. Not because I didn't wish to see them, but because I already had. Personal and professional tributaries in my life's course thus far had brought me to dozens of them in the past, and I knew, with varying degrees of intimacy and familiarity, Miami and Philadelphia, Washington and San Francisco, Dallas and Kansas City, Seattle and Atlanta, Denver and Tulsa, Charleston and Minneapolis, Phoenix and Buffalo, LA and Houston.

I didn't avoid cities because I don't love them. I love them abundantly, in all their glory and grime.

Traveling alone with kids wasn't a factor in building an itinerary that generally avoided cities. Dana and Adam have been at home in cities around the world, and they explore them as handily as they might a Scottish castle ruin in the Highlands or a sleepy Maltese village. At least once a year our family plunges into New York, where I was born, and Dana and Adam know Manhattan as a vibrant and wonderful friend. Cities play an important role in our family's travels.

In planning this trip, I had also reasoned that cities are destinations unto themselves. At any time, one can drive or fly to a good city, if only for a few days, and immerse oneself in it. The cities would be there after our road odyssey was over, places to pluck and taste and savor individually, each in its turn. Each was worth a trip of its own.

What I wanted to explore on this odyssey wasn't American cities, but everything in between them. America's smaller places and quieter landscapes.

And so, while the thought of a brilliant Chicago-right-down-there was exciting, it also hinted at the impending close of a journey that had been, intentionally, without cities. We had turned a geographic corner into a part of America that was strung with big, old, busy cities dense with people.

I sat on the sand at Manistique and reflected on some of the small, quiet, but iron-tough links in the great American chain we'd traveled along to get to this spot where Chicago sat right down there. This was an apt point to stop and gather up mental images of this long, magnificent journey's people and places, pasting their snapshots securely inside me somewhere so I would never lose them.

The whitewater rush of West Virginia rivers. The misty elegance of bluegrass dawn. The deep, green peace of the Natchez Trace. The haunting channels of Atchafalaya bayous. Thousand-foot cotton clouds sitting on an endless Texas. Pueblos and petroglyphs, mesas and mysteries of the country's first people. Deserts that demanded and rewarded hardiness and patience. Redwood forests whose fecund smell cloyed primally, sensually. Soaring mountains, hushed woods and fish-filled streams. Landscapes sculpted by glaciers and volcanoes. Prairies of dancing grass. And all the towns and villages, ranches and farms, Main Streets and neighborhoods, hamlets and ports, outposts and subdivisions, harbors and havens where people lived, worked, cried, enjoyed, believed, prayed, and welcomed us among them.

I turned my mind back to Chicago and was gripped with unease, the same small chill I sometimes felt now when I caught sight of Boston's two highest towers, skyscrapers that stand in the cityscape apart from the rest.

I had last been in Chicago several months before September 11. My plane left O'Hare and, before turning east to eventually offer views of Canada, Lake Ontario, Niagara Falls and the industrial cities that stretch in a straight line across upstate New York, the plane climbed out of Illinois by flying north over Lake Michigan, downtown Chicago sitting in its magnificent entirety right outside my window. The Sears Tower appeared so close and so powerfully high I imagined I could see people through its black glass windows. Then the plane banked just enough to reveal the silvery-blue Hancock tower. The whole city sat in a beautiful handful, her two tallest towers framing her, two sky-piercing exclamation points, statements of pride and hustle, spirit and muscle, hard work and big dreams.

But now, just a picture or thought of the Chicago skyline could unease me. The two towers didn't feel like exclamation points anymore. They were targets. Reminders. Symbols of all that had changed, so quickly, so brutally. The window seat view I had so lovingly inhaled in the spring of 2001 would now, I think, fill me with slight, sad fear. The view I had taken in then had embraced me. Now, I would want to reach down and embrace it. Gather it up, protect it, keep it safe. The city of big shoulders sits, arms open, heart exposed, vulnerable at the end of a long freshwater sea. No, it shall never be the same view again.

Route 2 took us east from Manistique, and the stretch near Brevort was stunning. Because we were on its north shore, Michigan was the only Great Lake we'd keep to starboard as we drove. The turquoise water lapped at white sand beaches that met the asphalt. Sometimes, the dunes were so close that, had Adam been a bit longer and lankier, he might have skimmed their sides with his hand as we rolled by. It was hard to keep driving. Much of the beach access was public, with state and federal lands combining to provide a limitless choice of beauty stops. People had pitched tents in the sand of campgrounds and forests, and looked forward to night music of campfire crackles and gently crashing waves.

St. Ignace (IG-ness), on the Straits of Mackinac (MAK-in-aw. All things Mackinac are pronounced MAK-in-aw, but only two, Fort Mackinaw and Makinaw City, are spelled that way. It took a while to get it straight.), sits at the northern end of Mighty Mac, the great bridge that links the Upper Peninsula to the rest of Michigan. The bridge also marks the meeting place of two colossal water bodies. As you stand in St. Ignace facing the bridge, the water to the right is Lake Michigan. The water to the left is Huron. We had met our third great lake.

We made ourselves very much at home at the motel formerly known as Big Chain Motel. Judy was there when we checked in, Judy was there into the night, and Judy was there when we left in the morning.

Judy was working two back to back seven to eleven shifts. Her sister had her two young kids for two days so Judy wouldn't have to worry about day care and so she could go home between shifts and catch a few hours sleep from midnight to six.

We loved this comfy place, and I told Judy, who practically ran it, that we appreciated all the touches and amenities that massaged some of the warrior out of people like us who'd been nearly a whole summer and ten thousand miles gone. There were free bikes that the kids rode around the parking lot, careful not to bump into the big golden moose outside the lobby door. A glorious heated indoor pool, connected visually and physically to the rest of the place, not stashed away in some mildewy basement. A homey lounge that felt like a living room, free popcorn at night, video games, big bowls of apples, lovely breakfast. You could walk around in your socks, just like at home. Pre- Big Chain, it was the

Motel DuPont, so named because of its proximity to the five mile-long suspension bridge that soared above the Straits.

Judy said they were looking to change franchises. "The chain is killing us. They've got five properties in Michigan, but only two in the U.P., and in Michigan, they're offering $40-$50 rates! We make all our money from June to August. They can't make us give it away for $50!" From June to August, St. Ignace is a gateway to Mackinac Island, the Nantucket or Catalina of the Great Lakes.

In the morning, I had to do a 5-miler before we boarded the ferry to Mackinac Island. The Motel DuPont, as Judy preferred it be called and hoped I would call it if I ever wrote about it, sat at the top of the access road to the Mackinac Bridge viewing area. I ran up and down the killer hill and sprinkled my 45 minutes with laps around the viewing area parking lot, empty at 6 a.m. except for maintenance men sweeping and mowing, and large groups of messy Canada geese. The lacy green and tan suspension bridge, art in steel, glowed mint in the sunrise as a nail polish-red barge passed beneath her. Great blue herons, gulls, and families of ducks graced the water and reeds I ran beside.

We said goodbye to Judy and boarded the Arnold Ferry that took us out into Lake Huron and delivered us in a half hour to Mackinac Island. The place was gorgeous, privileged, and overflowing with history and tourists. We rode big, fat-tired Schwinns, ate ice cream, bought postcards, and walked the streets, marveling at the boys whose summer job it is to shovel horse crap from the streets of this auto-free island into yellow plastic wheelbarrows. Where do they put it all? The great blooms that blossom all over the island, in gardens and window boxes, must be helped along because tourists ride horses and horse carts through the roads and lanes of Mackinac Island, a beautiful fake fairyland, so stunningly perfect and impeccable that it hurts. Teams of Belgian draft horses delivered Pepsi, Fruit Loops and bottled water to the island's inns and hotels. Hotel valet boys pedaled bicycles, piled high with luggage precariously perched in baskets, from the docks to the inns.

At the Grand Hotel, grand in this case being understatement, I tsk-tsked all the travel writers I'd read who'd written about this place, because they'd all left something out of their stories. The Grand Hotel, built after the Civil War in the opulent manner of resorts and refuges for the movers and shakers of the gilded age, boasts the world's longest front porch. I'd read about and seen photos of the porch for years, and Dana, Adam and I walked up the loftier than thou hill the hotel commands for the sole purpose of sitting in a rocking chair and looking out over the Straits.

But a quick rock in a wooden chair on the world's longest front porch costs 10 bucks a head if you're not a Grand Hotel guest, something the travel writers failed to report. The approach to the Grand is regal and, if you're not chic, moneyed, or willing to blow a chunk of the children's inheritance on a few nights here, rather intimidating. American flags and mango-yellow awnings lined the broad, tree-lined, uphill approach which was dotted with signs that, among other genteel but firm directives, told ladies they weren't allowed to wear "slacks." (Yikes! The planning of a trip here involves the packing of skirts!) The horse carriages of the rich and wish-they-weres clopped by, the carriage inhabitants wearing a hint of smile as they looked down on those of us on foot. The ye-who-are-not-registed-guests-must-pay-10-dollars-to-be-here signs started early, so you had the chance to hang it up and turn around, to forever wonder what lays at the top of that hill.

We made it, unimpeded, to the top of the driveway. The Grand truly was. We looked down on the garden lawn at the topiary and the registered guests playing croquet, the green Mackinac Bridge sitting beyond the lawn in the Straits, looking like the ultimate croquet hoop. We looked up at the great porch, most of the chairs empty and lined up, waiting for someone to sit in them and keep them company.

I saw two people in matching polo shirts. They were not smiling. I kept walking, looking at the superlative porch. I wanted to sit on it. I geared up for a challenge.

A polo shirt stopped me.

"Excuse me. Are you guests of the hotel?"

"No. We'd just like to sit on the porch for a minute."

"If you're not registered guests, there's a ten dollar per person fee to enter the property."

"Do you mean I really have to pay thirty dollars for my kids and I to just take a quick walk up there to the porch?"

"Yes."

"When I saw the signs along the driveway, I wondered how close we'd be able to get before someone stopped us. This must be the spot. From this point on, it costs ten bucks a head to walk on the hotel property?"

"Yes."

"So, this is the official line of demarcation. You're the border guards. On this side of you, free. On that side of you, ten bucks a head."

"Yes."

I laughed. We left. I loved and hated Mackinac Island.

The next morning, we drove onto the Mighty Mac. At the toll booth, a state trooper, legs spread and arms folded high across his chest, looked at and into every oncoming vehicle, ready to stop anyone he didn't like.


Crossing the span's five miles across the Straits of Mackinac was a geographic and psychological milestone. We had left the U.P. and were now in the mitten, and I announced to the kids that we were now more connected to, than separated from, home. From here, home was really just a good long ride away, had we wanted or needed to make it so. Once on the mitten, I felt connected to Ohio, which would lead, after a short dash through Pennsylvania's corner at Erie, to New York State, which, at this point, I thought of as being in our own backyard, a mere jaunt from our driveway.

When I was planning our route, and came to the map of Michigan's Lower Peninsula, I noticed a temptation. Because the map had forewarned me of the temptation before we ever left home, I was armed and ready to dodge it when I met it.

There was no doubt, I'd admitted to myself as I'd contemplated the one-dimensional paper map Michigan, that we would be road weary by the time we crossed the Straits. The kids might be bored. They might feel unbearable homesickness or longing to see their dad or friends. Or, worse, we might not be getting along. What if we'd stopped speaking to each other back in the High Plains? After traversing the continent in a small steel and fiberglass capsule, and then turning around and traversing it three-quarters more in the other direction, in a long, two-month span of slow 30, 40, or 50 mile-per-hour days along winding backroads and wooded byways, crowding together in motel rooms or a tent, and eating out of cans and boxes, we'd be feeling our collective limit start to kick in right around the thumb of the Michigan mitten.

Happily, because God blessed me with great kids, our August road reality was far rosier than this doomsday scenario. But I had indeed considered it.

And therein lay the temptation. The map told me, "Once you cross the Straits, you can end the trip quickly. From the end of the Mackinac Bridge, you can get home fast, and with just one left turn. Just take the interstate down to Detroit, then hook a left into Ontario. Take the fast freeway across to Hamilton, exit Canada at St. Catherines, and voila, you're back on the interstate in Buffalo, New York." Zoom, zoom. Just like that. Just like that, I could make Mackinac Island be the last place we really saw on this trip. I could neatly and efficiently dispense with everything that sat between St. Ignace and Boston.

Of course, this would be sacrilege, heresy, high travel treason. To sell out at the southern end of Mighty Mac would demean the value of the whole trip. The quest to explore America, to really see it, to feel the nation's strength and share her people's pride, to see where the country stood, to gauge it for ourselves, would be compromised if we omitted a large part of the nation from the sampling by racing through it on 70 mile-per-hour superhighways. And, the kids would think they'd seen the country when, in fact, I would have robbed them of significant pieces of it. With few exceptions, interstate rest areas don't tell you anything about a place.

Thus, the great interstate escape was, inherently, a tempting evil to be avoided. But the quick exit strategy had another corruption that made the resolution not to employ it imperative. It went into another country.

This trip was about America. On another trip, at another time, with another purpose, in other circumstances, I would not have hesitated to cross international borders, north or south. But this trip had to be pure. I felt so strongly about this that when the first iteration of a proposed route included El Paso, I resolved that we would not cross the border to shop in Ciudad Juarez. Had we gone to San Diego, we would not have visited Tijuana. Were Buffalo a stop, we'd have viewed the Falls only from the American side. It felt strange to make a decision which was so parochial, as I was used, in my life, to venturing as far afield as health, time, money, geopolitics and God's grace allowed, borders being formalities which, once crossed, led one to great new wonders. But, on this trip, crossing only borders between our own united states felt like the right decision, an important one, one I could not compromise.

One night, long after the trip, I picked up *River Horse* and began to read William Least Heat-Moon's account of all that had gone into the planning of his river voyage across America. One of the reasons it had taken him years to uncover a navigable water route was that he was searching for one that did not require long spells in border waters like the Great Lakes or Gulf of Mexico. "For my voyage," he wrote, "I wanted only an internal route across the nation." I read this passage over and over. I understood. His reasons may have been different, but the conviction was the same.

And so, from the end of Mighty Mac, we took the interstate as far as Gaylord, where we picked up winding, rural route 32 that rode us 65 miles back to the shores of Lake Huron.

We had some interstate fun on the way to Gaylord. I'd been thinking that Mackinac Island was the perfect honeymoon spot, and, as we drove off the bridge, serendipity delivered a pair of North Carolina newlyweds driving, presumably, south to home, having just, presumably, honeymooned on Mackinac. The car still had words and hearts with arrows painted all over it. Along with the usual Just Marrieds, the words "Hot Bride" were plastered all over the groom's side of the car. We pulled into a rest area at the same time as the recently united, and the kids and I watched to see whether a goddess would emerge from the passenger side. One did. The hot bride was a statuesque blond with patrician posture and aquiline features, nail polish and baby blue eye shadow applied to a perfect demure tease. Since she wasn't driving, and doubtless wouldn't be, she might not have seen the billing she was getting as her new husband chauffeured her through the country. I imagined unpleasantness at some future rest stop between the Rust Belt and Dixie when, unaware of the advertising hype, she might emerge from the car puffy-eyed, sans makeup, hair askew, or clothes rumpled, to the notice of some trucker who'd challenge her hotness. The groom was living dangerously.

Route 32 was a narrow, twisting, rural road that showed us little towns like Johannesberg, Vienna and Atlanta, "Elk Capital of Michigan!" where a stuffed elk under glass sat on the post office lawn. Adopt-a-Highway by the K-B Valley Mushroom Club.

The road brought us to Alpena, smack on Huron. I loved Alpena as soon as I saw the happy face on the city's sky blue water tower and Evergreen Cemetery's gleaming wrought iron fence, fresh-painted in vividly alive high-gloss emerald.

Alpena, "A Warm, Friendly Port," and home to cement plants sitting on the lakeshore, was remarkable in its ability to carry on gritty, necessary industry while making itself a beautiful, comfortable place to be and live. A balancing act perfectly executed. An economic base built on its position on the Great Lakes and a satisfying homey loveliness built on its position on the Great Lakes.

The little city's center held striking residential architecture, prosperous-looking, well-kept. A group of chocolate-colored rock-brick houses, one covered in vines from foundation to eaves. Victorians dressed in vivid colors with bold, eclectic trim work. The old downtown a perfect assemblage of brick and stone and brightly painted wood. Compared to most towns, which paint themselves shyly, Alpena's paint stores must carry an inordinate proportion of bright crayon box colors. Alpena celebrated itself exuberantly.

There were plenty of places to play and relax outdoors. Near downtown, Washington Avenue Park was a haven with a meandering pond and swaying marsh grasses. Parks and beaches lined Huron's shore. People played tennis at Bayview Park, next to the marina, the Alpena Yacht Club and an outdoor amphitheater where the audience had a view not only of the performers, but of Thunder Bay, the sandy shore, sailboats bobbing at anchor, the cement plant, the sign for glass-bottomed boat Shipwreck Tours, and two lighthouses, one a squat red metal structure and one tall and slender, painted white and mint green.

Two boys on bikes, helmets buckled on over baseball caps, rode up the marina gangway and hopped down into a dinghy from which they pulled rods and tackle boxes. They sped off to somewhere where the fish were biting, maybe the marshes and pond at Washington Avenue Park.

"You are an intrepid woman!" said Susan, as she pushed her chair back from the desk in the small office of her motel to get a better look at me and the kids. We liked each other instantly. She was a pistol with firecracker-red hair. She talked fast when she wanted to, slow when she wanted to, and she looked you right in the eye. Her drapy cotton clothes- loose trousers and shirt in a turquoise print more Maui than Michigan – were the sartorial equivalent of downtown Alpena's crayon-colored homes and businesses.

Susan sized us up and rented us a room, the $60 end unit closest to Lake Huron, with a bench outside. She wanted to know where we'd been, what we'd seen. She asked the kids what they thought of it all and smiled knowingly at the "It's okay," and "I like it. It's good." She looked back up at me and nodded. As I signed the credit card slip, she pushed her chair back again, and looked at the three of us. Then she looked Adam and Dana in the eye. "These are times you'll never get back with these kids," words aimed at all of us.

The motel sat on Huron on its own stretch of sand, and near the public beach at Mich-E-Ke-Wis Park. We saw Susan all the time, as she lived in a green cinderblock bunker-like structure to whose rear was attached the straight line of modest motel units, of which ours sat closest to Susan's personal space, closest to the lake. Susan's house, which looked homemade, was a beautiful thing to me. The funky bunker sat right on the beach and had a killer view of Thunder Bay, and Susan had a big rectangular window from which she could watch the moods of Lake Huron at all hours, in all seasons. I imagined a conversation that might have taken place years ago if Susan and her husband had, indeed, built this gloriously-sited home themselves. After tapping the last cinderblock into place and nailing down the roof, Susan might have said:

"We should paint it."

"What color?"

"Green."

"Dark green?"

"No, something wild and sea-foamy, like Huron all whipped up. I'll go find something." And then, I imagined her in the paint store, passing the quiet greens, and emerging with gallons of something called, maybe, Tropical Great Lakes Green, like the color of the Maui-Michigan pantsuit that worked so well with her blaze of orange hair.

We made the motel and the spaces and places near it our little universe. The kids were free to roam around, up to but not including stepping into Huron unless I was with them. There was plenty to keep them busy while I brought my journal up to date and did laundry. The park, the beach, a Dairy Queen, and, the mini-golf that I could see from our room's bathroom window. Every half hour or so, Adam, Dana or both would burst into the room (made into a commodious accommodation by the keep-door-open-park-New-Paint- right-outside method) and ask for more money for golf and video games. Adam spent a fortune in quarters in the arcade, trying to win a free round of golf. When they were all golfed out, we went to the beach, just as the lifeguards were calling it a day and packing up the rescue surfboard. At 7 p.m., it was still over 70 degrees, and a big ball of orange sun the color of Susan's hair still lit the calm, indigo water. "You can wade out there for quite awhile," she'd told me, "before you have to make any decisions." Dana, who'd been our official Great Lakes water temperature tester, pronounced Huron, "this part of it, anyway," the warmest of any she'd sampled.

Susan's big, logy dog had pooped on the little patch of grass that separated the motel parking lot from the beach, grass that served as a parking lot for her motorboat, the *Susan*. We picked our way around the boat and the dog droppings as we came and went. Susan saw our comings and goings and noticed the kids as they went back and forth between golf, ice cream and motel room TV.

"You have great kids."

"I do. Thanks for saying so. They are pretty cool. The kind of kids you can live in a minivan with for a whole summer. We've made it to Michigan, and we still like each other."

"I wish they'd gotten to see the turkey vultures we've had lately. Or the deer. I get deer on my lawn sometimes. And a great blue heron my husband calls Mister Blue. And, I hoped you'd be lucky enough to see a freighter. They call regularly, and it's quite impressive as they come into the bay."

I wished we'd seen all those things, too, and said so, but added, "The Dairy Queen, the mini-golf and the beach were enough for the kids. Just what the doctor ordered at this point in the trip. They had a lot of fun."

"The mini-golf is a good neighbor. Nice and quiet."

I told Susan I loved Alpena and felt lucky we'd come upon this fine place as we came into the homestretch of our American journey. It was a perfect near-ending, an ideal finishing touch. (Had we invoked the interstate escape clause when we'd reached the mitten, we would have missed it.) "I'll always remember Alpena. It's the kind of place I could live in."

Susan smiled and looked out at Huron. "People say kids from Alpena spend their first twenty years thinkin' about how to get out, and the next twenty years thinkin' about how to get back in."

Other people think about getting in, too. "We get lots of retirees movin' in, because it's cheap. They're all snowbirds. Drive their RVs to Arizona in the winter." She shook her head. "I can't see sittin' around in a lawn chair." No, Susan's ideal winter is spent right there in Alpena, watching out her big rectangular window for the Great Lakes freighters that anchor close to Thunder Bay to wait out the freeze in Superior. An ice cutter could make Alpena's Huron port accessible, but they don't bother, because "the water starts to flow again in February."

In the morning, I sat on the bench outside the room and laced up my running shoes in the still-dark, and, by the time I'd finished stretching, a glorious red-orange sun had started to ascend from the watery horizon. I ran to the orb's rising and watched it gain height, degree by degree, splashing magnificent shafts of colored light across Huron's surface as it climbed, slowly turning dawn to day. I watched it detach itself from the horizon and become a full and colossal tangerine, a blood orange hanging great and ripe over the gentle swells of the vast lake.

After the run, Susan caught me leaning against New Paint, stretching. "My, what a fit specimen." That made an old chick feel good. I'd loved her when she'd called me intrepid. Now, I wanted to take her home. She asked if we'd slept well.

"Slept well, and rose well. I just watched a magnificent sunrise."

She turned to the lake. "That's why we could never leave."


But we had to. We turned left out of Susan's driveway and onto Route 23, which would take us south to Ohio.

Just beyond the Alpena city limits, a sign announced, "You Are Now Crossing the 45th Parallel – Halfway Point Between the North Pole and the Equator."

Route 23 was schizophrenic. From Alpena to Bay City, where it began a temporary double life as I- 75 until Flint, it hugged the mitten's shore and rode us through all the simple, woodsy beach resort towns that line Saginaw Bay. This part of Route 23 was a journey through a landscape of modest motels and lakefront cabins, hideaways for hunters, fishermen and families on

summer vacation. Tall pines and swaths of beach, Dinosaur
Gardens, a giant whitewashed Jesus with a whole world in his
hands. Edibles on offer included Bay City Tomatoes, fish sausage
and jerky, Honey Rocks, cod, smelt, salmon, walleye, catfish and
whitefish, and deer, bear and buffalo jerky at Romeo's Party Store
in Tawas City.

A major personality change at Saginaw. From here, all the
way to Toledo, Route 23 was a straight and narrow stress-
inducing, truck-clogged nightmare. Walled in and breathed on by
trucks, trucks, trucks, all in a frantic, dangerous hurry. We were
either behind a truck and waiting to pass, or passing, but not quite
fast enough for the 18-wheeled monster behind us, hot and heavy
on our tailgate, his scary grill filling the rearview mirror like Jaws
getting ready to swallow us whole if we didn't HURRY UP AND
PASS, ALREADY, THEN GET THE HELL OUT OF THE
WAY! We hadn't been in such a maelstrom of roadway motion
since the Pennsylvania Turnpike near Scranton, nearly two
months ago. I'd grown unused to busy asphalt arteries, and
Saginaw to Toledo was a kinetic reminder of why I hadn't missed
them. I was able to take only one quick visual breather the whole
stretch, and the god of fun stuff timed things so that this one
moment of calm coincided with the moment we passed the
gigantic beef jerky outlet in Dundee that touted "34 FLAVORS"
and enticed you with a picture of a buffalo.


The Ohio border. A wave of nostalgia, for an odyssey not yet
over but soon to be, coursed through me. There was so little left
between here and our driveway, and what still remained was
practically a straight line. I had reached the last page of the Route
Narrative, and I could read its final few run-on sentences in one
eyeful.

Soon, all of the days of our odyssey into America would be behind us, with no more ahead to wonder about or look forward to. No more setting out with a new day's sun to find what the road would yield. All of the quest's days and everything they contained would exist only in the past tense, lived only through memory. Soon, we'd trade plans for reminiscences. Anticipation for accomplishment. Expectation for experiences. The exhilaration of discovery would be over, the destinations reached.

But, travel taken, like travel underway, has its own riches. By having reached what we'd set out to discover, we traded ignorance for knowledge, detachment for connection, separateness for understanding.

Implicit in nostalgia are both sadness and joy. Indeed, I'd begun grieving for something lost, something precious that can't be recaptured except through recollection. At the same time, alongside the bite of melancholy, sat a beautiful ache of happiness and gratitude. I thanked God for the wonder of this trip, for the gift of it. For the places we'd seen. For the people we'd met. For the little corners and quiet lives we'd been privileged to share. For the freedom, so undeniably ours, that the journey affirmed. For the health and means to undertake such travels. For the confirmation that America was filled, from border to border and shore to shore, with strong people whose proud colors flew true when times were tough. I damned September 11, but, without it, I might never have grasped what we were really made of.

I thanked God for this time with my children. Susan had put it just about right when she'd said, "these are times you'll never get back with these kids." And, I thanked God for Mike, a man who could miss his wife and kids for two months, and be thrilled for them every moment they were gone.

By the time we reached Port Clinton, a beautiful water town, I'd realized that the end of our trip was a good thing. It was time. While it was still in motion, it was bigger than we were, too big to grasp completely. It needed to be over to be wholly appreciated, considered, caressed, and valued as a life milestone. It needed to become memory to be fully alive.

The kids were less philosophical about reaching Ohio. As we crossed the state on Routes 2 and 6, they spent long hours communing with videos, CDs and Playstation. *Wayne's World 2*, which had enjoyed multiple showings in Texas and then again in Wisconsin, made a comeback between Toledo and Ashtabula.

The Ohio I saw – fields, barns and silos; stands selling white and bicolor corn, watermelons, tomatoes; signs proclaiming "Agriculture is Ohio's #1 Industry;" bait shops with leeches and shiners; boatyards and boat billboards; the shopkeeper's dumpster with the hand-painted plea, "NO FISH;" Erie-side wildlife refuges; floating fishing docks for rent on the Toussaint River; the eerie and seemingly under-defended cooling tower of the Davis-Besse Nuclear Power Station; giant plastics companies; the Ohio National Guard station; tree-ripened peaches; ferries moving between the Catawba Island peninsula and Erie's Bass Islands; the open-air church held in the Mon-Ami Winery parking lot ("Come As You Are") – all these passed to a backseat soundtrack of the ghost of Jim Morrison persuading Wayne and Garth to hold a Woodstockian rock concert in Aurora, Illinois, even though no bands had agreed to show up. An "if you build it, they will come" theme with Mike Myers and Dana Garvey as the Kevin Costner and Amy Madigan characters.

When a kid wearing headphones giggled to something I couldn't hear, I knew the Weird Al Yankovich tape was in play. I was contemplating rural Ohio, but Adam and Dana were one with Weird Al as he drove down the freeway in the fast lane with a rabid wolverine in his underwear.

Our Port Clinton motel didn't have a beach along its stretch of Erie, but it did have a concrete platform built over the water. We sat there into the evening with other motel guests, mostly families from the Midwest taking their week's summer vacation on the lake. We watched the inky, wind-tossed water, the dark humps of Middle Bass Island, the lavender-red sky, and the cooling towers of the nuclear power plant we'd passed earlier, sitting on the shore just west of us. "Devil's Tower," pronounced Dana.

Port Clinton, "Walleye Capital of the World," had a beautiful old downtown, vibrant and alive with residents and summer visitors. Exquisite brick buildings, like the old Island House, lined the main streets, and a procession of brick and clapboard mansions faced the lake.

In the morning, as the sun rose gray-yellow behind a veil of clouds that sat heavy on the lake's surface, I ran into town and watched the day's fishing and touring get under way. Two young boys, up and out before the sun, fished in the canal that ran beside the lakefront park. Fishing boats, filled to the gills with smiling, expectant tourists, set out from the marina for the 7 a.m. "Walk-On Fishin' Tours," and the drawbridge controller in the wood and Plexiglas booth raised or lowered the bridge according to the height of whatever was waiting to get through. The Port Clinton Fish Company was getting ready for another day of fish cleaning, and the bright yellow Island Rocket, still tied up at the dock, was preparing for the day's first trips to Put-in-Bay on Middle Bass.

Pushing east, with the pull of home seeping into our bones, we rode the low Thomas Edison Bridge over wide, lovely Sandusky Bay and looked down into its shallows and canals. Downtown Sandusky, a beautiful old brick place, had roads that shot from Main Street smack down into Lake Erie, a huge topiary clock gracing the city center, and neat wooden neighborhoods. Here, we picked up Route 6, which rode us, Erie to portside, until Cleveland.

A fascinating stretch of road, Route 6 ran through the hearts of dozens of vibrant and often beautiful Erie-side towns. The great lake was always close, and almost always visible, sometimes through trees or between houses. The towns closest to Sandusky were neat and modest. Those closest to Cleveland were affluent, filled with lakefront mansions of indescribable opulence. We rolled through the hearts of Huron, with its marina and huge ConAgra Harvest States Milling operation; little resort towns like Beulah Beach with cottages and motels and creeks that ran into Erie; Volunteer Bay with its mobile home parks; pretty Vermilion with its old downtown, canals and colorful harbor; and Lorain, a big, hard-working place that managed also to be beautiful. At Lorain's Ford van plant, ramps hung like tongues from the open rears of railcars that sat in the plant's yard, ready to slurp up the long lines of fresh vans and deliver them to dealers across the country.

After Lorain, the road assumed monikers like Erie and Clifton Avenues, more fitting addresses than Route 6 for the parade of palaces that lined the lakeshore from Lorain to Cleveland. Lake Erie lapped at the back lawns of these showplaces, which rivaled any collection of real estate wealth I have ever seen. Avon Lake, Bay Village, Rocky River, Lakewood. A sumptuous parade that led right into Cleveland. The stretch was punctuated with empty lakeshore lots, old mansions having been bulldozed to make way for bigger, better ones.

In Cleveland, the kids spent an hour walking around the Rock N' Roll Hall of Fame. I stayed in the lobby, to save having to shell out another $17 admission fee and to avoid having to turn a thousand dollars of Nikon equipment over to the kid working the coatroom. I passed the time watching fervent fans on pilgrimage grasp their tickets and descend the escalator into the shrine, and I read the inane messages hanging on the John Lennon Wish Tree. "To John: I wish I can be really smart and growth faster – Jane, Aug 5 2002." Sweet Jane needs more help than John can give her.

With Browns Stadium flashing "GOD BLESS AMERICA" in the rearview mirror, we left Cleveland on I-90. Near Erie, Pennsylvania, we left the Great Lakes and 11,500 miles of America behind us, and entered New York.

## 13

# *THE LONG, GREEN EXIT RAMP TO HOME:*
# *New York, Massachusetts*

Chautauqua Lake greeted us as we entered green New York. Chautauqua's summer life was in full swing, and people boated and floated, and sat on wooden Adirondack chairs on docks and decks and porches of old summer camps, cottages and marinas. We were on Route 17, and The Optimist Club of Jamestown had adopted-the-highway.

A sign at Salamanca, in both English and Seneca, a language of the Iroquoian family, told us we had entered the Seneca Nation. The Allegany Indian Reservation, one of three in the Seneca Nation, surrounds the Allegheny, a river whose name derives from Indian words for "long river" and "fine river." We crossed and recrossed the wide, twisting, forested Allegheny, and found it, indeed, both long and fine.

When you run your fingers and eyes over a map of western New York, peppered between the –burgs and –villes and –towns named for white settlers who moved in the 1700's from New England into the woods of this frontier to farm, raise livestock and run dairies, you see other names, older names, names that evoke the proud and quiet unity the six nations of the Iroquois Confederacy have with this land. The French and English used the terms Iroquois Confederacy and Six Nations, but the Seneca, Cayuga, Onondaga, Oneida, Mohawk and Tuscarora call themselves the Haudenosaunee. The map rings with the rich sounds of places like Geneseo, Gowanda, Cassadaga, Cattaraugus, Cohocton, Tioga, Owego, and Oneonta. When you're in the land,

187

if you slow down or stay still, you can feel a link to the woodlands' aboriginal people, whose territories are surrounded by the state of New York.

The Seneca, through whose land we rode, are one of the confederacy's "older brothers" and "Keepers of the Western Door." They, and the other nations, find themselves having to periodically remind the federal government of the 1794 Treaty of Canandaigua, executed by George Washington's first head of Indian affairs, Timothy Pickering, signed by fifty-nine sachems and war chiefs, including Ootaujeaugenh, Broken Axe, and Kenjauaugus, Stinking Fish, and witnessed by the Indians' Quaker friends to ensure that what was said was what was written. The two-century old treaty protects Haudenosaunee sovereignty and lands and has been used, recently, to legally challenge threats to either or both.

The towns we passed looked like postcards. Postcards you find in a soft cardboard tray on a table at a flea market or an antique store. Hand-tinted postcards that show old, rose-brick places, surrounded by green, on or near a river, nestled in hollows and valleys, and made of trim, wooden workingman houses and churches with tall, white steeples. The towns all looked safe and peaceful, tucked inside the soft, leafy hug of the land. Straight, neat Olean; Cuba, whose giant red cheese shop ships worldwide; Angelica, Hormell, full of traveler's services; Almond; Alfred, where Farmer Phil and Friends had adopted-a-highway and a university sat on a rise; hard-working Bath, 10 miles from Keuka, one of the Finger Lakes; and Campbell, home of Polly-O String Cheese.

At Corning, in Steuben County glass country, a new development of bright white houses sat on a hillside overlooking the road. "They look like cemetery headstones," I said.

"No they don't," said Adam, turning to consider them. "They look like the houses in one of those Christmas villages you put under your tree. Like Grandma and PopPop have. At night, they should put red light bulbs behind them all, and light them up like a Christmas village."

A huge, gleaming, red truck did a 15-point turn in our hotel parking lot before coming to rest along the side of the building. We weren't sure which driver or team's cars were housed inside the monster trailer, but we knew it'd be heading to the track at Watkins Glen, 20 minutes north on Seneca Lake, one of the longest of the Fingers. A major NASCAR race there had turned Corning into a fan-packed street festival. We found pasta at Sorge's, in business more than 50 years, then hung around with the racegoers on Market Street, which had been closed to traffic. We inhaled the smell of the sausages, beer, cigarettes and deep-fried stuff, the race crowd's staff of life. Outdoor grills and taps ran on overdrive, music blared, and marketers held raffles and sold products next to high testosterone racecars that lured lots of lookers. That night, after sending off my final newspaper story, which would run after we got home, I fell asleep, finally, to the irritated rasp of smoker's cough from the next room.

When we woke up in Corning, we woke to the trip's last day. We knew this would be the last day, as we'd discussed things, made decisions, and come to consensus. We would get up early and drive long. Eight hours. We'd agreed. And, we would skip two Route Narrative destinations.

"Cooperstown, I'd said. "The Baseball Hall of Fame. We can get up there, see it, and be back on the highway in a few hours. Plus, it's famous even without baseball. It's named for James Fenimore Cooper's family. *Last of the Mohicans*. Natty Bumpo ran around up there."

"I don't want to go," said Adam.

"Why not? You love baseball."

"I know. I just don't want to go right now."

"But it's the Baseball Hall of Fame."

"I know. I just don't want to go there now. I'd rather get home a day early."

Thus did Cooperstown get scratched from the Route Narrative. And Saratoga?

"Dane, Saratoga is so close to where we live. (Visualize Adam's head bobbing up and down.) If we go now, it will take an extra day to get home. (Visualize Adam's eyes rolling up into his head.) We've seen so many horses on this trip. (Visualize Adam turning to give Dana a stare that said, "yeah, like a zillion.") How about we save Saratoga for a weekend trip of its own, when racing season is in full swing, and everything is going on, and we can really be part of the whole scene?" I braced for a negotiation.

"Okay."

"What?"

"Okay. That's good. We can save it. We can go another time." (Visualize Adam sighing happily and readjusting his headphones.)

Before we pulled out of the Corning hotel parking lot, Adam took his finger and wrote "H O M E" and "M A S S" in the layers of American dust that sat thick on New Paint's rear window. On the tailgate, he etched "WASH ME," which New Paint wore with pride.

At Chemung, where we followed the river of the same name, Route 17 fairly sat on the Pennsylvania border, and the woods we looked into were across the state line. I thought of Tuscarora, the Allegheny we'd driven through in a tunnel when we'd crossed Pennsylvania so many moons and miles and memories ago. The Tuscarora were one of the six nations of Haudenosaunee. The invisible line between New York and Pennsylvania disappeared as a notion, and the land was one.

Also a summer ago, we'd crossed the Susquehanna, and here she was again. It seemed right that a river that figures so richly in American and Native American history should become, on this last day, an arc in the circle of our journey. She ran broad and green beside the road, fog playing on the ripples that trilled over her as she moved through the woods. Owego's crimson brick Historic District lined itself up along her bank, the white trim of the high, red, two-towered church catching pieces of sun.

Ten miles south of Albany, we crossed the Hudson on a sky-blue steel bridge. Full circle. We'd crossed her near Fishkill, New York, nearly 12,000 miles ago. Jetskiers played in the twinkling water below us. I pointed south. "If you followed that water, guys, in a few hours you'd be in New York harbor. You'd pass under the George Washington Bridge, you'd float by Grant's tomb and the *Intrepid*, and you'd come to the Statue of Liberty. Those jetskiers could ride to New York City if they wanted to." The kids liked the image. Jetskiing to New York City!

We saw the Massachusetts Turnpike's pilgrim hat logo and a sign that said "Boston." It was an odd moment. No one spoke for a while. We were almost home, and we didn't know what or how to feel.

We crossed the Massachusetts border at West Stockbridge, lush and rolling. After the bright blue "Massachusetts Welcomes You" sign near the Stockbridge tolls, I tooted the horn, and Adam and I rolled our windows down. We waved and whoopied at the cars lining up to go through the tollbooths. Some people had seen the tailgate etchings and had likely figured out we weren't crazy or rude, just long gone and now returning.

We passed the cellphone around and called all the people to whom the words, "We're in Massachusetts!" would mean something. Now they waited for us, while we rolled the final miles down the turnpike, which felt like a long, green exit ramp to home.

But we'd really been home all along.  Our whole journey had been a 12,000-mile discovery of home.

Somewhere out west, Dana had asked, "Sometimes you hear people are different.  Then you hear we're all the same.  Which is right?"

Both.  We have different ethnicities and backgrounds, different ways of making a living, different geographies and climates, different pastimes, different religions and traditions.

But we're also the same.  We love our families and communities.  We love our part of the country, but we respect the rest of it.  We work hard.  We're independent.  We cherish our freedom.  We speak our minds.  And, judging by the flags, patriotic symbols, and messages of hope and support that we saw everywhere across the land – on ranches and gas stations, logging trucks and billboards, fishing boats and bumper stickers, churches and diners – we share a love for this nation.

America exceeded my expectations.  No part of it failed me or left me empty.  It's a quilt of small, fascinating pieces that give great comfort when sewn together.  A kaleidoscope of beautiful shapes and colors that amaze when blended.

On any journey, whether short, long, or lasting whole relationships or lifetimes, you can usually find what you set out to discover.  You choose what to look for, what to focus on, what to celebrate.  I went on this trip looking for good things, and found great ones.

We neared our house.  New Paint rolled past our grocery store, the place she drives to most in normal life.  She probably wondered if there'd be another great road trip sometime in her future. I rubbed the callus on my driving finger. It was now hard as stone and the size of a quarter.

"How do you feel, mom?" asked Dana.

"Well, to paraphrase Chief Joseph, 'From where the sun now stands, I will drive no more forever.'"

Adam, Dana, and I held hands. I spoke. "Let's congratulate ourselves for what we've done." Our handclasp tightened. "Thank you both for making this trip one of the greatest experiences of my life. We've built memories that we all share now, that nothing can ever take away. They're ours. We earned them together."

We looked at and thanked one another. Then Adam patted my shoulder. "Great trip." Two words I will cherish always.

We turned up Bridge Street. One more corner, and we would see our house. "This feels strange!" said Dana. "My stomach feels funny." Adam and I nodded. We had the same homecoming butterflies.

We pulled up to the house, and Mike came out to greet us. Dana flew into his arms. Adam got out and waited in the street. Mike gave him a hug, then stood back and smiled. "You got tall, pal."

Printed in the United States
22703LVS00002B/106-132